JUNCTION
the
M25

CONTENTS

Junction Hopping Ltd

Published by
Junction Hopping Ltd
1st Edition
2001

Route explanations:

Find **JUNCTION** number you are approaching or wish to leave at, look up page number and direction either **(CLOCKWISE** or **ANTI-CLOCKWISE)**

ie. JUNCTIONS 1a-1b (CLOCKWISE) go to Page 1
JUNCTIONS 2-1a (ANTI-CLOCKWISE) go to Page 64

Type in BOLD CAPITALS - street or road name
ie. CROSSWAYS BOULEVARD

Type in <u>BOLD CAPITALS</u> - places to head for
ie. <u>DARTFORD</u>

Type in bold lower case represents Junctions and roundabouts or numbered instructions
ie. roundabout (3) or T Junction **or 3rd exit**

<u>JUNCTIONS 1a - 1b (CLOCKWISE)</u>

<u>Route 1</u> **<u>Roundabouts (5)</u>**

Drive across the **QUEEN ELIZABETH BRIDGE (A282)**
Keep in the left hand lane
Just as you pass through the Toll Booths leave at the **1st** slip-road
At the **1st roundabout** take the **3rd** exit into **COTTON LANE**
At the traffic lights turn right into **LONDON ROAD**
Continue into **THE BRENT (A226)**
At the **next roundabout (2)** take the **2nd** exit (straight ahead)
Continuing along **THE BRENT**
At the **mini-roundabout (3)** take the **1st** exit (turn left) into **PARK ROAD**
At the **next roundabout (4)** take the **1st** exit (turn left) into **PRINCES ROAD**
This leads to the **next roundabout (5)** which is Junction **1b** of the **M25**
<u>Follow the signs for the direction you wish to travel</u>

<u>Route 2</u> **<u>Roundabouts (11)</u>**

Drive across the **QUEEN ELIZABETH BRIDGE (A282)**
Keep in the left hand lane
Just as you pass through the Toll Booths leave at the **1st** slip-road
At the **1st roundabout** take the **2nd** exit (straight ahead) into **CROSSWAYS BOULEVARD (A206)**
At the **next roundabout (2)** take the **1st** exit (straight ahead)
At the **next roundabout (3)** take the **2nd** exit (straight ahead)
At the **next roundabout (4)** take the **2nd** exit (straight ahead)
Continuing along **CROSSWAYS BOULEVARD (A206)**
At the **next roundabout (5)** take the **2nd** exit (turn right) into **ST CLEMENT'S WAY**
At the **next roundabout (6)** take the **2nd** exit (straight ahead)
At the **next roundabout (7)** take the **1st** exit (straight ahead)
Keep in the left hand lanes following the signs for **<u>DARTFORD</u> (A296)**
At the **next roundabout (8)** take the **3rd** exit into **WATLING STREET**
At the **next roundabout (9)** take the **2nd** exit (straight ahead)
At the **next elongated roundabout (10)** take the **2nd** exit into **PRINCES ROAD**
This leads to the **next roundabout (11)** which is Junction **1b** of the **M25**
<u>Follow the signs for the direction you wish to travel</u>

<u>JUNCTIONS 1b - 2 (CLOCKWISE)</u>

<u>Route 1</u> **<u>Roundabouts (6)</u>**

Leave the **M25** at Junction **1b** follow the slip-road
At the **1st roundabout** take the **1st** exit (turn left) into **PRINCES ROAD**
At the **elongated roundabout (2)** take the **3rd** exit into **WATLING STREET**
At the **next roundabout (3)** take the **2nd** exit (straight ahead)
At the **next roundabout (4)** take the **2nd** exit (turn right) into **BEAN LANE**
At the **next roundabout (5)** take the **1st** exit (straight ahead)
Cross over the **A2** dual-carriageway
Keep to the left and follow the slip-road on to the **DARTFORD BY-PASS (A2)**
Once on the **A2** leave at the **1st** slip-road
This leads to the **next roundabout (6)** which is Junction **2** of the **M25**
<u>Follow the signs for the direction you wish to travel</u>

<u>Route 2</u> **<u>Roundabouts (5)</u>**

Leave the **M25** at Junction **1b** follow the slip-road
At the **1st roundabout** take the **3rd** exit (turn right) into **PRINCES ROAD**
At the **next roundabout (2)** take the **2nd** exit (straight ahead)
Continue through **4** sets of traffic lights
Turn left at the **5th** set of traffic lights (just past the garage)
This leads into **SHEPHERDS LANE**
At the **next roundabout (3)** take the **1st** exit (straight ahead) into **OLD BEXLEY LANE**
At the **next roundabout (4)** take the **1st** exit (turn left) on to the **DARTFORD BY-PASS (A2)**
Follow the signs for **<u>DOVER</u> (A2)**
Leave at the **1st** slip-road
This leads to the **next roundabout (5)** which is Junction **2** of the **M25**
<u>Follow the signs for the direction you wish to travel</u>

<u>Route 3</u> **<u>Roundabouts (2)</u>**

Leave the **M25** at Junction **1b** follow the slip-road
At the **1st roundabout** take the **2nd** exit (straight ahead) following the signs for the **M25**
Keep in the right hand lane
This leads to the **next roundabout (2)** which is Junction **2** of the **M25**
<u>Follow the signs for the direction you wish to travel</u>

<u>JUNCTIONS 2 - 3 (CLOCKWISE)</u>

<u>Route 1</u> **<u>Roundabouts (6)</u>**

Leave the **M25** at Junction **2** follow the slip-road
As you approach the roundabout keep to the right hand lane
Follow the signs for **<u>DARTFORD</u> (A225)**
At the **1st roundabout** take the **4th** exit back towards the **M25**
Keep in the left hand lane and leave at the **1st** slip-road
At the **next roundabout (2)** take the **1st** exit into **PRINCES ROAD**
At the **next roundabout (3)** take the **2nd** exit (straight ahead)
At the **2nd** set of traffic lights turn left into **LOWFIELD STREET (A225)**
Continue straight ahead into **HAWLEY ROAD (A225)**
Continue into **MAIN ROAD**
Continue into **DARTFORD ROAD (A225)**
At the **next roundabout (4)** take **3rd** exit into **GORSE HILL**
Continue into **LONDON ROAD**
At the **next roundabout (5)** take the **2nd** exit (straight ahead)
This leads to the **next roundabout (6)** which is Junction **3** on the **M25**
<u>Follow the signs for the direction you wish to travel</u>

<u>Route 2</u> **<u>Roundabouts (10)</u>**

Leave the **M25** at Junction **2** follow the slip-road
At the **1st roundabout** take the **3rd** exit following the signs **<u>LONDON</u> (A2)**
This leads to the **DARTFORD BY-PASS (A2)**
Leave at the **1st** slip-road
At the **next roundabout (2)** take the **1st** exit
At the **1st mini-roundabout (3)** take the **1st** exit into **OAKFIELD LANE**
At the **next roundabout (4)** take the **2nd** exit into **LEYTON CROSS ROAD**
At the **next roundabout (5)** take the **1st** exit (straight ahead) into **BIRCHWOOD ROAD**
At the **T** Junction (garage) turn left into **LONDON ROAD**
At the **mini-roundabout (6)** take the **1st** exit into **BARTHOLOMEW WAY**
At the **next mini-roundabout (7)** take the **2nd** exit (turn right)
At the **next mini-roundabout (8)** take the **1st** exit into **HIGH STREET**
At the **next mini-roundabout (9)** take the **1st** exit into **LONDON ROAD**
This leads to the **next roundabout (10)** which is Junction **3** of the **M25**
<u>Follow the signs for the direction you wish to travel</u>

JUNCTIONS 3 - 4 (CLOCKWISE)

Route 1 **Roundabouts (4)**

Leave the **M25** at Junction **3** at the **2nd** slip-road following the signs for the **SWANLEY** **(A20)**
At the **1st roundabout** take the **5th** exit on to the **SWANLEY BY-PASS (A20)** following the signs for **LONDON**
Continue on to **SIDCUP BY-PASS (A20)** and leave at the **1st** slip-road
At the **next roundabout (2)** take the **1st** exit into **SEVENOAKS WAY (A224)**
Continue straight ahead via **CRAY AVENUE** for **5** miles
Continuing via **COURT ROAD** following the signs for **SEVENOAKS (M25)**
At the **next roundabout (3)** take the **2nd** exit following the dual-carriageway
This leads to the **next roundabout (4)** which is Junction **4** of the **M25**
Follow the signs for the direction you wish to travel

Route 2 **Roundabouts (5)**

Leave the **M25** at Junction **3** at the **2nd** slip-road following the signs for the **SWANLEY** **(A20)**
At the **1st roundabout** take the **2nd** exit into **LONDON ROAD (A20)** following the signs for **FARNINGHAM**
At the **next roundabout (2)** take the **2nd** exit (straight ahead)
Continue into **GORSE HILL**
At the **next roundabout (3)** take the **2nd** exit (straight ahead)
Take the **1st** turning on the right into **EYNSFORD ROAD (A225)**
Following the signs for **EYNSFORD**
Continue into **HIGH STREET**
Continue into **STATION ROAD**
Continue under the railway bridge into **SHOREHAM ROAD**
Take the **1st** turning on the right into **CASTLE ROAD**
Continue into **REDMANS LANE**
Continue into **ROCK HILL**
Turn left into **JUBILEE ROAD**
Take the **1st** turning on the left into **HOLLY BUSH LANE**
At the crossroads continue straight ahead into **HEWITTS ROAD**
At the **next roundabout (4)** take the **1st** exit (turn left) on to the dual carriageway
This leads to the **next roundabout (5)** which is Junction **4** of the **M25**
Follow the signs for the direction you wish to travel

<u>JUNCTIONS 4 - 5 (CLOCKWISE)</u>

<u>Route 1</u> **<u>Roundabouts (4)</u>**

Leave the **M25** at Junction **4** follow the slip-road
At the **1st roundabout** take the **2nd** exit (turn right)
At the **next roundabout (2)** take the **1st** exit into the **ORPINGTON BY-PASS (A224)**
At the **next roundabout (3)** take the **2nd** exit (straight ahead) into **LONDON ROAD**
Continue into **POLHILL (A224)**
At the **mini-roundabout (4)** take the **2nd** exit into **SUNDRIDGE ROAD**
Continue into **CHEVENING ROAD**
At the traffic lights turn left into **MAIN ROAD (A25)**
This leads to Junction **5** of the **M25**
<u>Follow the signs for the direction you wish to travel</u>

<u>Route 2</u> **<u>Roundabouts (6)</u>**

Leave the **M25** at Junction **4** follow the slip-road
At the **1st roundabout** take the **2nd** exit (turn right)
At the **next roundabout (2)** take the **5th** exit into **HEWITTS ROAD**
At the crossroads turn right into **SHOREHAM LANE**
Continue into **CHELSFIELD LANE**
At the **T** Junction turn left into **SHACKLANDS ROAD**
Take the **1st** turning on the right into **HIGH STREET**
Take the **4th** turning on the left into **CHURCH STREET**
Continue into **STATION ROAD**
At the **T** Junction turn right into **SHOREHAM ROAD**
Continue into **STATION ROAD**
At the **next roundabout (3)** take the **1st** exit into **SEVENOAKS ROAD**
Continue into **OTFORD ROAD**
At the **1st mini-roundabout (4)** take the **2nd** exit (straight ahead)
At the traffic lights turn right into **BRADBOURNE VALE ROAD**
At the **next mini-roundabout (5)** take the **1st** exit (turn left)
At the **mini-roundabout (6)** take the **2nd** exit (turn right) into **WORSHIPS HILL**
Continue into **WESTERHAM ROAD**
This leads to Junction **5** of the **M25**
<u>Follow the signs for the direction you wish to travel</u>

JUNCTIONS 5 - 6 (CLOCKWISE)

Route 1 **Roundabouts (2)**

Leave the **M25** at Junction **5** follow the signs for **SEVENOAKS (A21)**
Keep to the right as you join the **A21** and take the **2nd** slip-road
Follow the signs for **WESTERHAM (A25)**
At the **T** Junction turn left into **WESTERHAM ROAD (A25)**
Continue into **MAIN ROAD**
Continue into **HIGH STREET**
Continue into **BRASTED ROAD**
Continue into **VICARAGE HILL**
Continue into **HIGH STREET**
Continue into **EAST HILL**
Continue into **GODSTONE ROAD**
Continue into **WESTERHAM ROAD**
Continue into **QUEBEC SQUARE**
Continue into **MARKET SQUARE**
Continue into **WESTERHAM ROAD**
Continue into **WEST HILL**
Continue into **OXTED ROAD**
At the **1st roundabout** take the **3rd** exit into **GODSTONE BY-PASS (A22)**
This leads to the **next roundabout (2)** which is Junction **6** of the **M25**
Follow the signs for the direction you wish to travel

Route 2 **Roundabouts (2)**

Leave the **M25** at Junction **5** follow the signs for **SEVENOAKS (A21)**
Leave at the **1st** slip-road into **WESTERHAM ROAD (A25)**
Take the **1st** turning on the left into **WESTERHAM ROAD**
Continue into **HOMEDEAN ROAD** (ignore no through road)
Take the **1st** turning on the left into **CHEVENING ROAD**
At the crossroads turn left continuing along **CHEVENING ROAD**
Take the **1st** turning on the right into **OVENDEN ROAD**
Continue up the hill and take the **1st** turning on the left into **PILGRIMS WAY**
At the **T** Junction turn right then turn immediate left
At the crossroads continue straight ahead
At the next crossroads turn right into **CLARKS LANE (B2024)**
At the **T** Junction turn right into **LIMPSFIELD ROAD**
Take the **2nd** turning on the left into **SLINES OAK ROAD** (pond on corner)
Keep right into **SLINES NEW ROAD**
At the **T** Junction turn right into **WOLDINGHAM ROAD**
At the **1st roundabout** take the **1st** exit into the **CATERHAM BY-PASS (A22)**
Continue straight ahead into **GODSTONE ROAD**
Continue into **GODSTONE HILL (A22)**
This leads to the **next roundabout (2)** which is Junction **6** of the **M25**
Follow the signs for the direction you wish to travel

JUNCTIONS 6 - 7 (CLOCKWISE)

Route 1 **Roundabouts (4)**

Leave the **M25** at Junction **6** follow the slip-road
At the **1st roundabout** take the **4th** exit into **GODSTONE HILL (A22)**
Continue into **GODSTONE ROAD (A22)**
At the traffic lights turn left continuing along **GODSTONE ROAD (B2030)**
At the **1st mini-roundabout (2)** take the **1st** exit into **STATION AVENUE**
Continue into **CHURCH HILL** Continue into **CHURCH ROAD**
Continue into **HIGH STREET**
At the **mini-roundabout (3)** take the **1st** exit into **CHALDON ROAD**
At the **mini-roundabout (4)** take the **1st** exit (straight ahead)
Continue into **ROOK LANE**
Continue into **DEAN LANE** and at the left hand bend take the **1st** turning on the right continuing along **DEAN LANE**
At the **T** Junction turn left into **BRIGHTON ROAD (A23)**
This leads on to the **M23** which leads to Junction 7 of the **M25**
Follow the signs for the direction you wish to travel

Route 2 **Roundabouts (2)**

Leave the **M25** at Junction **6** follow the slip-road
At the **1st roundabout** take the **2nd** exit into **GODSTONE HILL (B2235)**
At the **next roundabout (2)** take the **3rd** exit (straight ahead) into **HIGH STREET**
Continue into the one way system and keep to the right
Take the **1st** turning on the right into **GODSTONE GREEN ROAD**
Then turn left into **BLETCHINGLEY ROAD (A25)**
Continue into **GODSTONE ROAD**
Take the **2nd** turning on the right into **CHURCH LANE**
Continue into **PLACE FARM ROAD**
Turn right into **WHITEHILL LANE**
Continue over the **M23**
Take the **1st** turning on the left into **SPRING BOTTOM LANE**
At the **T** Junction turn right into **HILL TOP LANE**
At the next **T** Junction turn left into **ROOK LANE**
Continue into **DEAN LANE**
Take the **1st** turning on the right continuing along **DEAN LANE**
At the **T** Junction turn left into **BRIGHTON ROAD (A23)**
This leads on to the **M23** which leads to Junction 7 of the **M25**
Follow the signs for the direction you wish to travel

JUNCTIONS 7 - 8 (CLOCKWISE)

Route 1 **Roundabouts (1)**

Leave the **M25** at Junction 7 follow the signs for **CROYDON (M23)**
Follow the **1st** slip-road then take the right-hand slip-road
This leads into **BRIGHTON ROAD (A23)**
At the **1st** set of traffic lights (garage) turn left into **STAR LANE**
Take the **2nd** turning on the left
At the crossroads continue straight ahead into **HOGSCROSS LANE**
At the next crossroads turn left into **HIGH ROAD**
Continue into **BLACKHORSE LANE**
At the **T** Junction turn left into **BRIGHTON ROAD (A217)**
Cross over to the right hand lanes
This leads to the **1st roundabout** which is Junction **8** of the **M25**
Follow the signs for the direction you wish to travel

Route 2 **Roundabouts (1)**

Leave the **M25** at Junction 7 following the signs for **CROYDON (M23)**
Follow the **1st** slip-road then take the right-hand slip-road
This leads into **BRIGHTON ROAD (A23)**
Take the **1st** turning on the right into **DEAN LANE**
Keep right continuing along **DEAN LANE**
At the **T** Junction turn right into **ALDERSTEAD LANE**
Continue into **SHEPHERD'S HILL (B2031)**
At the next **T** Junction turn left into **LONDON ROAD NORTH (A23)**
Take the **2nd** turning on the right (filter road) into **GATTON BOTTOM**
At the main **T** Junction turn right into **REIGATE HILL (A217)**
Following the signs for the **M25**
This leads to the **1st roundabout** which is Junction **8** of the **M25**
Follow the signs for the direction you wish to travel

JUNCTIONS 8 - 9 (CLOCKWISE)

Route 1 **Roundabouts (5)**

Leave the **M25** at Junction **8** follow the slip-road
At the **1st roundabout** take the **4th** exit into **BRIGHTON ROAD (A217)**
At the **next roundabout (2)** take the **1st** exit (straight ahead)
At the **next roundabout (3)** take the **1st** main exit (straight ahead)
Take the **1st** turning on the left into **MILL ROAD** follow the signs for **TADWORTH**
At the crossroads continue straight ahead into **NEW ROAD (B290)**
At the **T** Junction turn left into **MERE ROAD** Continue into **WALTON STREET**
Take the **3rd** turning on the right past the pond into **EBBISHAM LANE**
Keep left into **HURST ROAD**
At the **T** Junction turn right into **WALTON ROAD**
At the next **T** Junction turn right into **HEADLEY ROAD**
Continue into **FARM LANE** and at the **T** Junction turn left into **EPSOM ROAD**
Continue into **THE STREET** Continue into **LEATHERHEAD ROAD (A24)**
At the **next roundabout (4)** take the **3rd** exit on to the **(A243)**
This leads to the **next roundabout (5)** which is Junction **9** of the **M25**
Follow the signs for the direction you wish to travel

Route 2 **Roundabouts (5)**

Leave the **M25** at Junction **8** follow the slip-road
At the **1st roundabout** take the **1st** exit into **REIGATE HILL (A217)**
Continue along **LONDON ROAD** Continue into **CASTLEFIELD ROAD**
Turn right into **CHURCH STREET** Continue into **HIGH STREET**
Keep in the left hand lane and continue into **WEST STREET (A25)**
Continue into **BUCKLAND ROAD** Continue into **MAIN ROAD**
Continue into **REIGATE ROAD**
At the **next roundabout (2)** take the **3rd** exit into **STATION ROAD (B2032)**
Continue into **PEBBLE HILL ROAD (B2032)**
Continue into **DORKING ROAD**
Take the **1st** turning on the left into **HEADLEY COMMON ROAD**
Take the **3rd** turning on the left following the signs for **LEATHERHEAD**
Continue into **LEECH LANE (B2033)** Continue into **MILL WAY**
Continue into **REIGATE ROAD**
At the **next roundabout (3)** take **3rd** exit into **LEATHERHEAD BY-PASS RD**
At the **next roundabout (4)** take the **2nd** exit (straight ahead)
This leads to the **next roundabout (5)** which is Junction **9** of the **M25**
Follow the signs for the direction you wish to travel

JUNCTIONS 9 - 10 (CLOCKWISE)

Route 1 **Roundabouts (5)**

Leave the **M25** at Junction **9** follow the slip-road
At the **1st roundabout** take the **3rd** exit on to the **LEATHERHEAD BY-PASS ROAD (A243)**
At the **next roundabout (2)** take the **2nd** exit (straight ahead) into **OXSHOTT ROAD (A244)**
At the **next roundabout (3)** take the **2nd** exit (straight ahead) into **LEATHERHEAD ROAD (A244)**
Continue into **HIGH STREET**
Continue into **WARREN LANE** Continue into **COPSEM LANE**
At the **next roundabout (4)** take the **1st** exit into **ESHER BY-PASS (A3)**
Continue on the **PORTSMOUTH ROAD (A3)**
Follow the signs for the **M25** and leave at the **2nd** slip-road
This leads to the **next roundabout (5)** which is Junction **10** of the **M25**
Follow the signs for the direction you wish to travel

Route 2 **Roundabouts (9)**

Leave the **M25** at Junction **9** follow the slip-road
At the **1st roundabout** take the **2nd** exit into **LEATHERHEAD BY-PASS ROAD**
At the **next roundabout (2)** take the **2nd** exit (turn right) into **KINGSTON ROAD (B2430)**
At the **next roundabout (3)** take the **3rd** exit (straight ahead)
At the **next roundabout (4)** take the **2nd** exit (straight on) into **OXSHOTT ROAD**
At the **T** Junction turn left continuing **OXSHOTT ROAD (A244)**
At the **next roundabout (5)** take the **1st** exit (turn left) into **OAKLAWN ROAD**
At the **T** Junction turn right into **WOODLANDS ROAD (A245)**
Continue into **WOODLANDS LANE (A245)**
At the **T** Junction turn right into **STOKE ROAD (A245)**
Continue into **MILL ROAD** Continue into **HIGH STREET**
Continue into **BETWEEN STREETS**
At the **next roundabout (6)** take the **1st** exit on to **PORTSMOUTH ROAD**
At the **next roundabout (7)** take the **1st** exit (straight ahead) continuing along **PORTSMOUTH ROAD**
At the **next roundabout (8)** take the **1st** exit (turn left) into **PORTSMOUTH ROAD (A3)**
Follow the signs for the **M25** and leave at the **1st** slip-road
This leads to the **next roundabout (9)** which is Junction **10** of the **M25**
Follow the signs for the direction you wish to travel

JUNCTIONS 10 - 11 (CLOCKWISE)

Route 1 **Roundabouts (11)**

Leave the **M25** at Junction **10** follow the slip-road
At the **1st roundabout** take the **3rd** exit on to **PORTSMOUTH ROAD (A3)**
Leave at the **1st** slip-road **(PAINSHILL JUNCTION)**
At the **next roundabout (2)** take the **1st** exit into **BYFLEET ROAD (A245)**
At the **1st** set of traffic lights turn right into **SEVEN HILLS ROAD (B365)**
At the **next roundabout (3)** take the **2nd** exit (straight ahead)
At the **triangular roundabout (4)** take the **1st** exit into **QUEENS ROAD (A317)**
At the **next roundabout (5)** take the **2nd** exit (turn right)
At the **next roundabout (6)** take the **1st** exit (turn left) into **MONUMENT HILL**
Continue into **HIGH STREET** Continue into **CHURCH STREET**
At the **next roundabout (7)** take the **3rd** exit (turn right) into **BALFOUR ROAD**
At the **next roundabout (8)** take the **1st** exit (straight ahead) into **WEYBRIDGE ROAD (A317)**
At the **next roundabout (9)** take the **2nd** exit (straight on) into **WOBURN HILL**
At the **next roundabout (10)** take the **2nd** exit into **ST PETER'S WAY (A317)**
This leads to the **next roundabout (11)** which is Junction **11** of the **M25**
Follow the signs for the direction you wish to travel

Route 2 **Roundabouts (8)**

Leave the **M25** at Junction **10** follow the slip-road
At the **1st roundabout** take the **1st** exit on to **PORTSMOUTH ROAD (A3)**
When you are on the **A3** leave at the **1st** slip-road
At the **next roundabout (2)** take the **2nd** exit into **PORTSMOUTH ROAD**
Continue into **HIGH STREET**
Take the **1st** turning on the right into **NEWARK LANE (B367)**
Continue into **THE PARADE** Continue into **CHURCH HILL (B367)**
Turn right into **UPSHOTT LANE** following the signs for **BYFLEET**
Continue into **COLDHARBOUR ROAD** Continue into **OAKCROFT ROAD**
At the **T** Junction turn left into **OLD WOKING ROAD**
At the **next roundabout (3)** take the **2nd** exit into **SHEERWATER ROAD (A245)**
At the **next roundabout (4)** take the **1st** exit into **WOODHAM LANE (A245)**
Take **1st** turning on the right into **MARTYR'S LANE**
At the **next roundabout (5)** take the **3rd** exit into **GUILDFORD ROAD (A320)**
At the **next roundabout (6)** take the **2nd** exit (straight ahead)
At the **next roundabout (7)** take the **2nd** exit into **ST PETER'S WAY (A320)**
This leads to the **next roundabout (8)** which is Junction **11** of the **M25**
Follow the signs for the direction you wish to travel

JUNCTIONS 11 - 12 (CLOCKWISE)

Route 1 **Roundabouts (6)**

Leave the **M25** at Junction **11** follow the slip-road
At the **1st roundabout** take the **1st** exit into **ST PETERS WAY (A320)**
At the **next roundabout (2)** take the **1st** exit into **GUILDFORD ROAD (A320)**
At the **next roundabout (3)** take the **3rd** exit into **CHOBHAM ROAD (A319)**
Continue into **CHERTSEY ROAD (A319)**
At the T Junction turn left into **HIGH STREET**
At the **1st mini-roundabout (4)** take the **2nd** exit into **BAGSHOT ROAD (A319)**
At the **next roundabout (5)** take the **3rd** exit into **GUILDFORD ROAD**
Continue into **LIGHT WATER BY-PASS (A322)**
This leads to the **next roundabout (6)** take the **3rd** exit on to the **M3**
Follow the signs for **LONDON** then leave at the **1st** slip-road
This leads to Junction **12** of the **M25**
Follow the signs for the direction you wish to travel

Route 2 **Roundabouts (9)**

Leave the **M25** at Junction **11** follow the slip-road
At the **1st roundabout** take the **3rd** exit into **ST PETERS WAY (A317)**
At the **next roundabout (2)** take the **1st** exit into **CHERTSEY ROAD (A317)**
Continue straight ahead into **FORDWATER ROAD (B387)**
Continue into **WEIR ROAD**
At the traffic lights turn right into **BRIDGE ROAD (B375)**
Continue into **CHERTSEY BRIDGE ROAD**
At the **next roundabout (3)** take the **2nd** exit into **CHERTSEY ROAD (B375)**
Continue into **RENFREE WAY**
At the **next roundabout (4)** take the **2nd** exit into **RUSSELL ROAD (A375)**
At the **1st mini-roundabout (5)** take the **1st** exit (straight ahead)
At the **next roundabout (6)** take the **1st** exit into **GASTON BRIDGE ROAD**
At the **next roundabout (7)** take the **2nd** exit (straight ahead)
Continue into **UPPER HALLIFORD BY-PASS (A224)**
At the **next roundabout (8)** take the **1st** exit into **UPPER HALLIFORD ROAD**
Continue into **WINDMILL ROAD**
At the main traffic lights (shears interchange) turn right into **STAINES ROAD WEST (A308)**
At the **next roundabout (9)** take the **5th** exit on to the **M3** following the signs for **PORTSMOUTH**
Leave at the **1st** slip-road this leads to Junction **12** of the **M25**
Follow the signs for the direction you wish to travel

JUNCTIONS 12 - 13 (CLOCKWISE)

Route 1 **Roundabouts (4)**

Leave the **M25** at Junction **12** follow the slip-road
Keep to the right following the signs for **LONDON** **M3** once on the **M3** leave the **M3** at the **1st** slip-road which is Junction **1** of the **M3**
At the **1st roundabout** take the **1st** exit into **STAINES ROAD WEST (A308)**
Continue into **KINGSTON ROAD (A308)**
At the **next roundabout (2)** take the **2nd** exit (straight ahead) into **STAINES BY-PASS (A308)**
At the **next roundabout (3)** take the **2nd** exit continuing along the **STAINES BY-PASS (A30)**
This leads to the **next roundabout (4)** which is Junction **13** of the **M25**
Follow the signs for the direction you wish to travel

Route 2 **Roundabouts (5)**

Leave the **M25** at Junction **12** follow the slip-road
Keep to the left following the signs for **PORTSMOUTH** **M3** once on the **M3** leave the **M3** at the **1st** slip-road which is Junction **3** of the **M3**
At the **1st roundabout** take the **3rd** exit into **BRACKNELL ROAD (A322)**
Continue through the traffic lights
Then take the **2nd** turning on the left following the signs for **LONDON** **(A30)**
At the **T** Junction turn left into **LONDON ROAD (A30)**
At the **next roundabout (2)** take the **2nd** exit (straight ahead) into **LONDON ROAD** and follow for approximately **5** miles
Continue into **EGHAM HILL**
At the **next roundabout (3)** take the **2nd** exit into **EGHAM BY-PASS (A30)**
At the **next roundabout (4)** take the **2nd** exit on to the **A30**
This leads to the **next roundabout (5)** which is Junction **13** of the **M25**
Follow the signs for the direction you wish to travel

<u>JUNCTIONS 13 - 14 (CLOCKWISE)</u>

<u>**Route 1**</u> <u>**Roundabouts (3)**</u>

Leave the **M25** at Junction **13** follow the slip-road
Following the signs for <u>**STAINES**</u> **(A30)**
At the **1st roundabout** take the **3rd** exit into **STAINES BY-PASS (A30)**
Keep to the left hand lane
At the traffic lights turn left
Then turn left into **STANWELL MOOR ROAD (A3044)**
At the **next roundabout (2)** take the **1st** exit into **AIRPORT WAY (A3113)**
This leads to the **next roundabout (3)** which is Junction **14** of the **M25**
<u>**Follow the signs for the direction you wish to travel**</u>

<u>**Route 2**</u> <u>**Roundabouts (4)**</u>

Leave the **M25** at Junction **13** follow the slip-road
At the **1st roundabout** take the **1st** exit into **(B376)**
At the **next roundabout (2)** take the **3rd** exit (turn right) into **WRAYSBURY ROAD**
Continue into **STAINES ROAD (B376)**
Continue into **HIGH STREET**
Continue into **STATION ROAD**
Continue into **COPPERMILL ROAD**
At the **T** Junction turn right into **STANWELL ROAD**
Continue into **HORTON ROAD**
At the **next roundabout (3)** take the **2nd** exit (straight ahead) continuing along **HORTON ROAD**
This leads to the **next roundabout (4)** which is Junction **14** of the **M25**
<u>**Follow the signs for the direction you wish to travel**</u>

<u>JUNCTIONS 14 - 15 (CLOCKWISE)</u>

<u>Route 1</u> **<u>Roundabouts (7)</u>**

Leave the **M25** at Junction **14** follow the slip-road
At the **1st roundabout** take the **3rd** exit into **AIRPORT WAY (A3113)**
At the **next roundabout (2)** take the **1st** exit into **STANWELL MOOR ROAD (A3044)**
At the **next roundabout (3)** take the **2nd** exit (straight ahead)
At the traffic lights turn right into **COLNBROOK BY-PASS**
At the next traffic lights turn left into **HATCH LANE** following the signs for **<u>WEST DRAYTON</u> (A3044)**
At the **1st mini-roundabout (4)** take the **3rd** exit (turn right) into **HOLLOWAY LANE**
At the **mini-roundabout (5)** take the **2nd** exit (straight ahead)
At the **next roundabout (6)** take the **2nd** exit (straight ahead)
A t the traffic lights turn right following the signs for the **M4 M25**
At the **next roundabout (7)** take the **3rd** exit on to the **M4**
Once on the **M4** leave at the **1st** slip-road
This leads to Junction **15** of the **M25**
<u>Follow the signs for the direction you wish to travel</u>

<u>Route 2</u> **<u>Roundabouts (3)</u>**

Leave the **M25** at Junction **14** follow the slip-road
At the **1st roundabout** take the **1st** exit into **HORTON ROAD** following the signs for **<u>POYLE</u>**
At the **next roundabout (2)** take the **1st** exit (straight ahead) continuing along **HORTON ROAD**
Continue into **STANWELL ROAD**
Take the **3rd** turning on the right into **HORTON ROAD** following the signs for **<u>COLNBROOK</u>**
Follow the hairpin bend into **HIGH STREET**
Continue into **LONDON ROAD**
At the **T** Junction continue straight ahead into **LONDON ROAD (A4)**
At the **next roundabout (3)** take the **4th** exit on to the **M4**
Following the signs for **<u>LONDON</u>**
Once on the **M4** leave at the **1st** slip-road
This leads to Junction **15** of the **M25**
<u>Follow the signs for the direction you wish to travel</u>

JUNCTIONS 15 - 16 (CLOCKWISE)

Route 1 **Roundabouts (6)**

Leave the **M25** at Junction **15** follow the slip-road
Once on the **M4** keep left following the signs for **SLOUGH** **M4**
Leave at the **1st** slip-road which is Junction **5** of the **M4**
At the **1st roundabout** take the **4th** exit into **LONDON ROAD (A4)**
Continue into **SUSSEX PLACE** Continue into **WELLINGTON STREET**
Keep to the left at the **next roundabout (2)** (traffic lights) and take the **3rd** exit (turn right) into **UXBRIDGE ROAD (A412)**
At the **next roundabout (3)** take the **2nd** exit into **CHURCH ROAD (A412)**
At the **1st mini-roundabout (4)** take the **2nd** exit (straight ahead)
At the **next mini-roundabout (5)** take the **1st** exit into **DENHAM ROAD**
This leads into Junction **1** of the **M40**
At the **next roundabout (6)** take the **1st** exit (turn left) then turn **1st** left on to **M40**
Once on the **M40** leave at the **1st** slip-road this leads to Junction **16** of the **M25**
Follow the signs for the direction you wish to travel

Route 2 **Roundabouts (9)**

Leave the **M25** at Junction **15** follow the slip-road
Then keep in the right hand lane on to the **M4** following the signs for **LONDON**
Once on the **M4** leave at the **1st** slip-road
At the **1st roundabout** take the **1st** exit (filter lane) into **STOCKLEY ROAD (A408)** then keep in the right hand lane of the Dual carriageway
At the **next roundabout (2)** continue straight ahead
At the **next roundabout (3)** take the **2nd** exit (straight ahead) into **PARK VIEW ROAD (A408)**
At the **next roundabout (4)** take the **2nd** exit continuing into **FALLING LANE**
At the traffic lights turn right into **HIGH STREET (A408)**
Continue into **HIGH ROAD** Continue into **HIGH STREET**
At the **next roundabout (5)** take the **2nd** exit (straight ahead)
Continue into **COWLEY ROAD**
At the **next roundabout (6)** take the **2nd** exit into **OXFORD ROAD (A4020)**
At the **next roundabout (7)** take the **1st** exit (straight ahead)
Follow the signs for the **M40** this leads into Junction **1** of the **M40**
At the **next roundabout (8)** take the **1st** exit
At the **next roundabout (9)** take the **2nd** exit (straight ahead)
Take the **1st** turning on the left on to the **M40** following the signs for **OXFORD**
Once on the **M40** leave at the **1st** slip-road this leads to Junction **16** of the **M25**
Follow the signs for the direction you wish to travel

<u>JUNCTIONS 16 - 17 (CLOCKWISE)</u>

<u>Route 1</u> **<u>Roundabouts (4)</u>**

Leave the **M25** at Junction **16** follow the **2nd** slip-road
Following the signs for **<u>LONDON</u> M40**
Once on the **M40** leave at the **1st** slip-road
At the traffic lights turn left
At the **1st roundabout** take the **1st** exit (turn left) into **OXFORD ROAD (A40)**
Keep in the right hand lane
At the **1st** set of traffic lights turn right into **DENHAM AVENUE (A412)** following the signs for **<u>WATFORD</u>**
Continue into **DENHAM WAY**
At the **next roundabout (2)** take the **2nd** exit (straight ahead) continuing along **DENHAM WAY**
At the **next roundabout (3)** take the **1st** exit (filter lane) on to the **A412**
This leads to the **next roundabout (4)** which is Junction **17** of the **M25**
<u>Follow the signs for the direction you wish to travel</u>

<u>Route 2</u> **<u>Roundabouts (6)</u>**

Leave the **M25** at Junction **16** follow the **2nd** slip-road
Following the signs for **<u>LONDON</u> M40**
Once on the **M40** leave at the **1st** slip-road
At the traffic lights turn left
At the **1st roundabout** take the **1st** exit into **OXFORD ROAD (A40)**
At the **2nd** set of traffic lights turn right into **AMERSHAM ROAD (A413)** following the signs for **<u>THE CHALFONTS</u>**
Continue into **CHALFONT ST PETER BY-PASS (A413)**
At the **next roundabout (2)** take the **2nd** exit (straight ahead)
At the **next roundabout (3)** take the **3rd** exit (turn right) into **JOINER'S LANE**
At the **T** Junction turn left into **DENHAM LANE**
Take the **1st** turning on the right into **WEST HYDE LANE**
Continue into **SHIRE LANE**
Continue into **CHALFONT LANE**
At the **next roundabout (4)** take the **1st** exit (turn left) into **DENHAM WAY (A412)**
At the **next roundabout (5)** take the **1st** exit (filter lane) on to the **A412**
This leads to the **next roundabout (6)** which is Junction **17** of the **M25**
<u>Follow the signs for the direction you wish to travel</u>

JUNCTIONS 17 - 18 (CLOCKWISE)

Route 1 **Roundabouts (4)**

Leave the **M25** at Junction **17** follow the slip-road
At the **1st roundabout** take the **3rd** exit into **DENHAM WAY (A412)**
At the **next roundabout (2)** take the **1st** exit into **UXBRIDGE ROAD (A412)**
At the **next roundabout (3)** take the **1st** exit into **RECTORY ROAD**
At the **next roundabout (4)** take the **1st** exit into **CHORLEYWOOD ROAD (A404)**
This leads to Junction **18** of the **M25**
Follow the signs for the direction you wish to travel

Route 2 **Roundabouts (1)**

Leave the **M25** at Junction **17** follow the slip-road
At the **1st roundabout** take the **1st** exit (turn left) into **LONG LANE**
Take the **3rd** turning on the right into **STAG LANE**
Continue into **BERRY LANE**
Continue under the bridge
Then take the **1st** turning on the left into **DOG KENNEL LANE**
At the traffic lights turn right into **RICKMANSWORTH ROAD (A404)**
This leads to Junction **18** of the **M25**
Follow the signs for the direction you wish to travel

JUNCTIONS 18 - 20 (CLOCKWISE)

Route 1 **Roundabouts (8)**

Leave the **M25** at Junction **18** follow the slip-road
At the traffic lights turn right into **CHORLEYWOOD ROAD (A404)**
At the **1st roundabout** take the **1st** exit into **PARK ROAD**
At the **next roundabout (2)** take the **2nd** exit (straight ahead)
Continue into **SCOTS HILL (A412)**
At the 1st mini-roundabout (3) take the **2nd** exit into **WATFORD ROAD (A412)**
At the **next roundabout (4)** take the **2nd** exit (straight ahead)
At the **next roundabout (5)** take the **1st** exit into **RICKMANSWORTH ROAD**
Keep in the left hand lane
At the **next roundabout (6)** take the **1st** exit (turn left)
Follow the one way system which leads into **HEMPSTEAD ROAD (A411)**
Following the signs for the **M25**
At the **next roundabout (7)** take the **2nd** exit (straight ahead) into **WATFORD ROAD (A41)**
This leads to the **next roundabout (8)** which is Junction **20** of the **M25**
Follow the signs for the direction you wish to travel

Route 2 **Roundabouts (1)**

Leave the **M25** at Junction **18** follow the slip-road
At the traffic lights turn left into **RICKMANSWORTH ROAD (A404)**
At the next set of traffic lights turn right into **SOLESBRIDGE LANE**
Keeping left
At the **T** Junction turn right into **SARRATT ROAD**
Take the **1st** turning on the left into **REDHALL LANE**
Continue into **FIR TREE HILL**
Keep left into **LANGLEYBURY LANE**
At the traffic lights turn left into **WATFORD ROAD (A41)**
This leads to the **next roundabout (1)** which is Junction **20** of the **M25**
Follow the signs for the direction you wish to travel

<u>JUNCTIONS 19 - 20 (CLOCKWISE)</u>

<u>**Route 1**</u>   <u>**Roundabouts (2)**</u>

Leave the **M25** at Junction **19** follow the slip-road
At the **1st roundabout** take the **1st** exit into **WATFORD ROAD (A41)**
This leads to the **next roundabout (2)** which is Junction **20** of the **M25**
<u>**Follow the signs for the direction you wish to travel**</u>

<u>JUNCTIONS 19 - 21 (CLOCKWISE) (for the M1 Northbound)</u>

Only use if you intend to leave the M25 at Junction 21 for the M1 <u>North</u>

<u>**Route 1**</u>   <u>**Roundabouts (4)**</u>

Leave the **M25** at Junction **19** follow the slip-road
At the **1st roundabout** take the **2nd** exit into **NORTH WESTERN AVENUE**
Keep in the left hand lane and leave at the **1st** slip-road
At the **next roundabout (2)** take the **2nd** exit into **KINGSWAY NORTH ORBITAL ROAD (A405)** following the signs for **M25**
At the **elongated roundabout (3)** continue straight ahead continuing along **KINGSWAY NORTH ORBITAL ROAD (A405)**
Continue into **NORTH ORBITAL ROAD (A405)**
At the **next elongated roundabout (4)** take the **1st** exit (turn left) on to the **M1** following the signs **M1 <u>NORTH</u>** this leads to Junction **21** of the **M25**
<u>**Follow the signs for the direction you wish to travel**</u>

<u>JUNCTIONS 19 - 21a (CLOCKWISE)</u>

Only use if you wish to continue on the M25 or you are leaving at Junction 21a

<u>**Route 1**</u>   <u>**Roundabouts (4)**</u>

Leave the **M25** at Junction **19** follow the slip-road
At the **1st roundabout** take the **2nd** exit into **NORTH WESTERN AVENUE**
Keep in the left hand lane and leave at the **1st** slip-road
At the **next roundabout (2)** take the **2nd** exit into **KINGSWAY NORTH ORBITAL ROAD (A405)** following the signs for the **M25**
At the **elongated roundabout (3)** continue straight ahead continuing along **KINGSWAY NORTH ORBITAL ROAD (A405)**
Continue into **NORTH ORBITAL ROAD (A405)**
At the **next elongated roundabout (4)** continue straight ahead along **NORTH ORBITAL ROAD (A405)**
This leads to the **next roundabout (4)** which is Junction **21a** of the **M25**
<u>**Follow the signs for the direction you wish to travel**</u>

JUNCTIONS 20 - 21 (M1 NORTH)

You should only use Route 1 if you intend to leave the M1 at Junction 21 for the M1 Northbound

Route 1 **Roundabouts (5)**

Leave the **M25** at Junction **20** follow the slip-road
At the **1st roundabout** take the **4th** exit on to **WATFORD ROAD (A41)**
At the **next roundabout (2)** take the **1st** exit into **NORTH WESTERN AVENUE**
Keep in the left hand lanes and leave at the **1st** slip-road
At the **next roundabout (3)** take the **2nd** exit into **KINGSWAY NORTH ORBITAL ROAD (A405)**
At the **elongated roundabout (4)** continue straight ahead still in **KINGSWAY NORTH ORBITAL ROAD (A405)**
Continue into **NORTH ORBITAL ROAD (A405)**
At the **next elongated roundabout (5)** take the **1st** exit (turn left) on the **M1 NORTHBOUND**
This leads to Junction **21** of the **M25**
Follow the signs for the direction you wish to travel

If you use Route 2 you cannot leave the M25 at Junction 21a the 1st exit is Junction 22

Route 2 **Roundabouts (10)**

Leave the **M25** at Junction **20** follow the slip-road
At the **1st roundabout** take the **1st** exit into the **BERKHAMSTED BY-PASS**
Leave at the **1st** slip-road following the signs for **HEMEL HEMPSTEAD**
At the **next roundabout (2)** take the **2nd** exit (turn right)
At the **next roundabout (3)** take the **1st** exit into **TWO WATERS ROAD (A414)**
At the **1st mini-roundabout (4)** take the **2nd** exit (turn right)
At the **2nd mini-roundabout (5)** take the **1st** exit (keep left)
At the **3rd mini-roundabout (6)** take the **2nd** exit into **ST ALBANS ROAD**
At the **next roundabout (7)** take the **1st** exit (straight ahead)
At the **next roundabout (8)** take the **2nd** exit (straight ahead)
At the **next roundabout (9)** take the **2nd** exit into **BREAKSPEAR WAY (A414)**
At the **next roundabout (10)** take the **2nd** exit (straight ahead)
This leads to Junction **8** of the **M1** follow the signs for **M1 SOUTHBOUND**
Once on the **M1** leave at the **2nd** slip-road
This leads to Junction **21** of the **M25**
Follow the left hand slip-road this leads on to the **M25 EASTBOUND**
Follow the signs for the direction you wish to travel

JUNCTIONS 20 - 21a (CLOCKWISE)

Route 1 **Roundabouts (6)**

Leave the **M25** at Junction **20** follow the slip-road
At the **1st roundabout** take the **4th** exit on to **WATFORD ROAD (A41)**
At the **next roundabout (2)** take the **1st** exit into **NORTH WESTERN AVENUE**
Keep in the left hand lane and leave at the **1st** slip-road
At the **next roundabout (3)** take the **2nd** exit into **KINGSWAY NORTH ORBITAL ROAD (A405)**
At the **elongated roundabout (4)** continue straight ahead still in **KINGSWAY NORTH ORBITAL ROAD (A405)**
Continue into **NORTH ORBITAL ROAD (A405)**
At the **next elongated roundabout (5)** continue straight ahead along **NORTH ORBITAL ROAD (A405)**
This leads to the **next roundabout (6)** which is Junction **21a** of the **M25**
Follow the signs for the direction you wish to travel

Route 2 **Roundabouts (14)**

Leave the **M25** at Junction **20** follow the slip-road
At the **1st roundabout** take the **1st** exit into the **BERKHAMSTED BY-PASS (A41)**
Leave at the **1st** slip-road following the signs for **HEMEL HEMPSTEAD**
At the **next roundabout (2)** take the **2nd** exit (turn right)
At the **next roundabout (3)** take the **1st** exit into **TWO WATERS ROAD (A414)**
At the **1st mini-roundabout (4)** take the **2nd** exit (turn right)
At the **2nd mini-roundabout (5)** take the **1st** exit (keep left)
At the **3rd mini-roundabout (6)** take the **2nd** exit into **ST ALBANS ROAD (A414)**
At the **next roundabout (7)** take the **1st** exit (straight ahead)
At the **next roundabout (8)** take the **2nd** exit (straight ahead)
At the **next roundabout (9)** take the **2nd** exit into **BREAKSPEAR WAY (A414)**
At the **next roundabout (10)** take the **2nd** exit this leads to Junction **8** of the **M1**
Continue straight ahead this leads on to the **M1 SOUTHBOUND**
Once on the **M1** leave at the **1st** slip-road this leads on to the **M10**
At the **next roundabout (11)** take the **4th** exit into **NORTH ORBITAL ROAD**
At the **next roundabout (12)** take the **2nd** exit (straight ahead)
At the **next roundabout (13)** take the **1st** exit (straight ahead)
This leads to the **next roundabout (14)** which is Junction **21a** of the **M25**
Follow the signs for the direction you wish to travel

JUNCTIONS 21 - 21a (CLOCKWISE)

Route 1 **Roundabouts (5)**

Leave the **M25** at Junction **21** joining the **M1** **NORTHBOUND**
Leave the **M1** at the **1st** slip-road this is Junction **8** of the **M1**
Keep left into **BREAKSPEAR WAY**
At the **1st roundabout** take the **4th** exit (a U-turn) this leads to Junction **8** of the **M1**
Continue straight ahead following the signs for **M1** **SOUTHBOUND**
Once on the **M1** leave at the **1st** slip-road this leads on to the **M10**
At the **next roundabout (2)** take the **4th** exit into **NORTH ORBITAL ROAD (A405)**
At the **next roundabout (3)** take the **2nd** exit (straight ahead)
At the **next roundabout (4)** take the **1st** exit (straight ahead) following the signs for **M25**
This leads to the **next roundabout (5)** which is Junction **21a** of the **M25**
Follow the signs for the direction you wish to travel

JUNCTIONS 21 - 22 (CLOCKWISE)

Route 1 **Roundabouts (4)**

Leave the **M25** at Junction **21** joining the **M1** **NORTHBOUND**
Leave the **M1** at the **1st** slip-road this is Junction **8** of the **M1**
Keep left into **BREAKSPEAR WAY**
At the **1st roundabout** take the **4th** exit (U-turn) this leads to Junction **8** of the **M1**
Continue straight ahead following the signs for **M1** **SOUTHBOUND**
Once on the **M1** leave at the **1st** slip-road which is Junction 7 of the **M1** which leads on to the **M10**
At the **next roundabout (2)** take the **2nd** exit on to **NORTH ORBITAL ROAD (A414)**
At the **next roundabout (3)** take the **3rd** exit on to **LONDON COLNEY BY-PASS (A1081)** following the signs for the **M25**
This leads to the **next roundabout (4)** which is Junction **22** of the **M25**
Follow the signs for the direction you wish to travel

JUNCTIONS 21a - 22 (CLOCKWISE)

Route 1 **Roundabouts (6)**

Leave the **M25** at Junction **21a** follow the slip-road
At the **1st roundabout** take the **1st** exit into **NORTH ORBITAL ROAD (A405)**
At the **next roundabout (2)** take the **2nd** main exit (ignore the hotel entrance)
At the **next roundabout (3)** take the **2nd** exit (straight ahead)
At the **next roundabout (4)** take the **3rd** exit into **NORTH ORBITAL ROAD (A414)**
At the **next roundabout (5)** take the **3rd** exit into **LONDON COLNEY BY-PASS (A1081)** following the signs for the **M25**
This leads to the **next roundabout (6)** which is Junction **22** of the **M25**
Follow the signs for the direction you wish to travel

Route 2 **Roundabouts (6)**

Leave the **M25** at Junction **21a** follow the slip-road
At the **1st roundabout** take the **1st** exit into the **NORTH ORBITAL ROAD (A405)**
At the **next roundabout (2)** take the **3rd** main exit (U-turn) into **NORTH ORBITAL ROAD (A405)**
Then take the **1st** turning on the left into **LYE LANE**
At the **T** Junction turn left continuing along **LYE LANE**
At the next **T** Junction turn right into **STATION ROAD**
Continue over the bridge
Take the **1st** turning on the left into **SMUG OAK LANE**
At the **T** Junction turn right into **RADLETT ROAD (B5183)** follow for **1** mile and take the **1st** turning on the left into **HARPER LANE (B556)**
At the **next roundabout (3)** take the **2nd** exit (straight ahead) into **BELL LANE**
At the **next roundabout (4)** take the **2nd** exit (straight ahead)
At the **next roundabout (5)** take the **1st** exit (turn left) over the **M25** following the signs for **HARLOW (M25)**
This leads to the **next roundabout (6)** which is Junction **22** of the **M25**
Follow the signs for the direction you wish to travel

JUNCTIONS 22 - 23 (CLOCKWISE)

Route 1 **Roundabouts (6)**

Leave the **M25** at Junction **22** follow the slip-road
At the **1st roundabout** take the **5th** exit back over the **M25**
At the **next roundabout (2)** take the **1st** exit into **ST ALBANS ROAD (B556)**
Continue until you reach **SOUTH MIMMS**
At the **next roundabout (3)** take the **2nd** exit into **ST ALBANS ROAD**
At the **next roundabout (4)** take the **2nd** exit this leads into **SOUTH MIMMS SERVICES**
At the **next roundabout (5)** continue into **BIGNELL'S CORNER** following the signs for the **M25 DARTFORD TUNNEL**
This leads to the **next roundabout (6)** which is Junction **23** of the **M25**
Follow the signs for the direction you wish to travel

Route 2 **Roundabouts (5)**

Leave the **M25** at Junction **22** follow the slip-road
At the **1st roundabout** take the **3rd** exit into **COURSERS ROAD**
At the **next roundabout (2)** take the **3rd** exit (turn right) into **TOLLGATE ROAD**
Cross over the Motorway
Then take the **1st** turning on the right into **SWANLAND ROAD**
At the **next roundabout (3)** take the **1st** exit into **ST ALBANS ROAD** this leads into **SOUTH MIMMS SERVICES**
At the **next roundabout (4)** continue into **BIGNELL'S CORNER** following the signs for the **M25 DARTFORD TUNNEL**
This leads to the **next roundabout (5)** which is Junction **23** of the **M25**
Follow the signs for the direction you wish to travel

JUNCTIONS 23 - 24 (CLOCKWISE)

Route 1   **Roundabouts (5)**

Leave the **M25** at Junction **23** follow the slip-road
At the **1st roundabout** take the **2nd** exit into the **SOUTH MIMMS SERVICES**
At the traffic lights turn left into **SWANLAND ROAD** following the signs for **SOUTH MIMMS**
At the **next roundabout (2)** take the **1st** exit into **ST ALBANS ROAD**
At the **next roundabout (3)** take the **2nd** exit (turn right) into **CECIL ROAD**
Continue into **MUTTON LANE (B556)**
At the **1st mini-roundabout (4)** take the **2nd** exit (straight ahead)
Keep in the middle lane
Continue straight ahead through the traffic lights
Continue into **SOUTHGATE ROAD (A111)** following the signs for the **M25**
This leads to the **next roundabout (5)** which is Junction **24** of the **M25**
Follow the signs for the direction you wish to travel

Route 2   **Roundabouts (2)**

Leave the **M25** at Junction **23** follow the slip-road
At the **1st roundabout** take the **4th** exit into **ST ALBANS ROAD (A1081)**
Take the **1st** turning on the left into **DANCERS HILL ROAD**
At the **T** Junction turn right into **BARNET ROAD (A1000)**
Take the **1st** turning on the left into **WAGON ROAD**
Continue into **WAGGON ROAD**
At the **T** Junction turn left into **STAGG HILL**
Continue into **COCKFOSTERS ROAD (A111)**
This leads to the **next roundabout (2)** which is Junction **24** of the **M25**
Follow the signs for the direction you wish to travel

JUNCTIONS 24 - 25 (CLOCKWISE)

Route 1 **Roundabouts (2)**

Leave the **M25** at Junction **24** follow the slip-road
At the **1st roundabout** take the **3rd** exit into **THE RIDGEWAY (A1005)**
Take the **1st** turning on the left into **EAST LODGE LANE**
At the **T** Junction turn right into **CATTLEGATE ROAD**
Follow into **THEOBALDS PARK ROAD**
Then take the **1st** turning on the left into **WHITEWEBBS ROAD**
Continue into **WHITEWEBBS LANE**
Continue into **BULLS CROSS** (bearing right)
At the Junction turn left into **BULLSMOOR LANE**
At the traffic lights turn left into **GREAT CAMBRIDGE ROAD (A10)**
This leads to the **next roundabout (2)** which is Junction **25** of the **M25**
Follow the signs for the direction you wish to travel

Route 2 **Roundabouts (9)**

Leave the **M25** at Junction **24** follow the slip-road
At the **1st roundabout** take the **1st** exit (turn left) into **SOUTHGATE ROAD (A111)**
A t the traffic lights turn right into **HIGH STREET**
At the **4th** set of traffic lights keep right into **THE CAUSEWAY** (avoid right hand turn) following the signs for CUFFLEY **(B156)**
Continue into **COOPER'S LANE**
Continue into **JUDGE'S HILL**
At the **1st mini-roundabout (2)** continue straight ahead into **NORTHAW ROAD WEST (B516)**
At the **next mini-roundabout (3)** continue (straight ahead)
Continue into **NORTHAW ROAD EAST (B156)**
At the **next mini-roundabout (4)** take the **2nd** exit (straight ahead)
Take the **1st** turning on the right into **STATION ROAD**
At the **next-mini-roundabout (5)** continue straight ahead into **CUFFLEY HILL**
At the **next mini-roundabout (6)** take the **2nd** exit into **GOFF'S LANE**
At the **next roundabout (7)** take the **3rd** exit (turn right) into **LIEUTENANT ELLIS WAY**
At the **next roundabout (8)** take the **3rd** exit (turn right) into **GREAT CAMBRIDGE ROAD (A10)**
This leads to the **next roundabout (9)** which is Junction **25** of the **M25**
Follow the signs for the direction you wish to travel

JUNCTIONS 25 - 26 (CLOCKWISE)

Route 1 **Roundabouts (8)**

Leave the **M25** at Junction **25** follow the slip-road
At the **1st roundabout** take the **1st** exit into **GREAT CAMBRIDGE ROAD (A10)**
At the **next roundabout (2)** take the **3rd** exit into **WINSTON CHURCHILL WAY**
At the **next roundabout (3)** take the **3rd** exit into **HIGH STREET (A121)**
Continue into **MONARCHS WAY**
At the **next roundabout (4)** take the **1st** exit (straight ahead) into **ELEANOR CROSS ROAD (A121)**
Continue into **STATION ROAD**
At the traffic lights turn right following the signs for the **M25, A121**
At the **next roundabout (5)** take the **2nd** exit (straight ahead) **(A121)**
At the **next roundabout (6)** take the **2nd** exit (straight ahead) **(A121)**
At the **next roundabout (7)** take the **2nd** exit into **HONEY LANE** following the signs **M11, M25**
This leads to the **next roundabout (8)** which is Junction **26** of the **M25**
Follow the signs for the direction you wish to travel

Route 2 **Roundabouts (7)**

Leave the **M25** at Junction **25** follow the slip-road
At the **1st** roundabout take the **3rd** exit into the **GREAT CAMBRIDGE ROAD (A10)** following the signs for **ENFIELD (A10)**
At the **1st** set of traffic lights turn left into **BULLSMOOR LANE (A1055)**
Continue into **MOLLISON AVENUE**
At the **next roundabout (2)** take the **2nd** exit (straight ahead)
At the **next roundabout (3)** take the **2nd** exit (straight ahead)
At the **next roundabout (4)** take the **1st** exit into **VALLEY ROAD (A110)**
At the main traffic lights turn left into **SEWARDSTONE ROAD (A112)**
At the **next roundabout (5)** take the **3rd** exit (turn right) following the signs for the **A121, M25**
At the **next roundabout (6)** take the **2nd** exit into **HONEY LANE** following the signs **M11, M25**
This leads to the **next roundabout (7)** which is Junction **26** of the **M25**
Follow the signs for the direction you wish to travel

JUNCTIONS 26 - 27 (CLOCKWISE)

Route 1 **Roundabouts (5)**

Leave the **M25** at Junction **26** follow the slip-road
At the **1st roundabout** take the **3rd** exit (turn right) into **HONEY LANE (A121)**
At the **next roundabout (2)** take the **1st** exit continuing along **HONEY LANE**
Continue into **WOODRIDDEN HILL (A121)**
At the **next roundabout (3)** take the **4th** exit into **EPPING NEW ROAD (A104)**
At the **next roundabout (4)** take the **2nd** exit (straight ahead)
Continue into **WOODFORD GREEN**
Continue into **HIGH ROAD (A11)**
At the one way system follow right then take the **1st** turning on the left into **WOODFORD NEW ROAD (A104)**
At the **next roundabout (5)** take the **1st** exit into **SOUTHEND ROAD (A406)**
This leads into Junction **4** of the **M11**
Keep in the middle lane when you are on the **NORTH CIRCULAR ROAD**
Take the **1st** slip-road on to the **M11** following the signs for the **M11** **CAMBRIDGE**
Leave at the **2nd** slip-road following the signs for the **M25**
This is Junction **6** of the **M11** which is also Junction **27** of the **M25**
Follow the signs for the direction you wish to travel

Route 2 **Roundabouts (6)**

Leave the **M25** at Junction **26** follow the slip-road
At the **1st roundabout** take the **3rd** exit (turn right) into **HONEY LANE (A121)**
At the **next roundabout (2)** take the **1st** exit continuing along **HONEY LANE**
Continue into **WOODRIDDEN HILL (A121)**
At the **next roundabout (3)** take the **1st** exit into **EPPING ROAD (B1393)**
Continue into **HIGH ROAD**
Continue into **HIGH STREET**
At the **1st mini-roundabout (4)** take the **1st** exit (straight ahead)
At the **next mini-roundabout (5)** take the **2nd** exit (straight ahead) into **PALMERS HILL**
At the traffic lights continue straight ahead into **THORNWOOD ROAD**
Continue into **HIGH ROAD (B1393)**
Continue into **LONDON ROAD**
At the **next roundabout (6)** take the **5th** exit on to the **M11** **SOUTHBOUND** following the signs for **M25**
Leave at the **1st** slip-road this leads to Junction **27** of the **M25**
Follow the signs for the direction you wish to travel

JUNCTIONS 27 - 28 (CLOCKWISE)

Route 1 **Roundabouts (4)**

Leave the **M25** at Junction **27** follow the slip-road
Then follow the right hand slip-road and the signs for **LONDON (M11)**
Once on the **M11** leave the **M11** at Junction **4** keeping to the left hand lane following the signs for **ROMFORD (A12)**
Leave at the next slip-road
At the **1st roundabout** take the **2nd** exit into **EASTERN AVENUE (A12)**
At the **next roundabout (2)** take the **3rd** exit following the signs for **ROMFORD**
Continuing along **EASTERN AVENUE (A12)**
Continue into **EASTERN AVENUE WEST (A12)**
Continue into **EASTERN AVENUE EAST (A12)**.
As you approach the signs for **BRENTWOOD (A12)** keep in the left hand lane
Do not continue over the flyover (Gallows corner)
At the **next roundabout (3)** take the **2nd** exit into **COLCHESTER ROAD (A12)**
Leave at the slip-road following the signs for **M25**
This leads to the **next roundabout (4)** which is Junction **28** of the **M25**
Follow the signs for the direction you wish to travel

Route 2 **Roundabouts (6)**

Leave the **M25** at Junction **27** follow the slip-road
Then follow the left hand slip-road and the signs for **CAMBRIDGE M11**
Once on the **M11** leave at the **1st** slip-road
At the **1st roundabout** take the **4th** exit into **CANES LANE (A414)**
At the **next roundabout (2)** take the **1st** exit (straight ahead)
At the **next roundabout (3)** take the **2nd** exit into **EPPING ROAD (A414)**
At the **next roundabout (4)** take the **3rd** exit into **HIGH STREET (A128)**
Continue into **COOPER'S HILL**
At the **next roundabout (5)** take the **1st** exit into **BRENTWOOD ROAD (A128)**
Continue into **ONGAR ROAD**.
When you reach **BENTLEY** pass the garage and turn right into **MORES LANE**
At the **T** Junction turn left then immediate right into **LINCOLNS LANE**
At the next **T** Junction turn left into **WEALD ROAD**
Then take the **1st** turning on the right into **WIGLEY BUSH LANE**
At the traffic lights turn right into **BROOK STREET (A1023)**
This leads to the **next roundabout (6)** which is Junction **28** of the **M25**
Follow the signs for the direction you wish to travel

JUNCTIONS 28 - 29 (CLOCKWISE)

Route 1 **Roundabouts (2)**

Leave the **M25** at Junction **28** follow the slip-road
At the **1st roundabout** take the **2nd** exit into **BROOK STREET (A1023)**
At the **1st** set of traffic lights turn right into **NAGS HEAD LANE**
At the **T** Junction turn right then immediate left into **HALL LANE**
At the next **T** Junction turn right
Then continue left on to the **SOUTHEND ARTERIAL ROAD (A127)**
Leave at the **1st** slip-road (**3rd** on the left) following the signs for **M25**
This leads to the **next roundabout (2)** which is Junction **29** of the **M25**
Follow the signs for the direction you wish to travel

Route 2 **Roundabouts (2)**

Leave the **M25** at Junction **28** follow the slip-road
At the **1st roundabout** take the **2nd** exit into **BROOK STREET (A1023)**
At the **2nd** set of traffic lights turn right into **MASCALLS LANE**
At the **next** set of traffic lights turn right into **WARLEY ROAD (B186)**
Continue into **GREAT WARLEY STREET (B186)**
Cross over the **SOUTHEND ARTERIAL ROAD (A127)**
Then take the **1st** turning on the left on to the **SOUTHEND ARTERIAL ROAD (A127)** following the signs for **LONDON**
Leave at the **1st** slip-road following the signs for the **M25**
This leads to the **next roundabout (2)** which is Junction **29** of the **M25**
Follow the signs for the direction you wish to travel

JUNCTIONS 29 - 30 (CLOCKWISE)

Route 1 **Roundabouts (7)**

Leave the **M25** at Junction **29** follow the slip-road
At the **1st roundabout** take the **1st** exit into the **SOUTHEND ARTERIAL ROAD**
Once on the **A127** leave at the **1st** slip-road
At the **T** Junction turn right into **WARLEY STREET (B186)**
Cross over the dual-carriageway and continue into **ST MARY'S LANE**
At the **1st mini-roundabout (2)** take the **1st** exit (turn left) into **CLAY TYE ROAD (B186)** continuing into **OCKENDON ROAD (B186)**
Continue into **NORTH ROAD** Continue into **SOUTH ROAD**
At the **next mini-roundabout (3)** take the **2nd** exit (straight ahead)
At the **next mini-roundabout (4)** take the **1st** exit (straight ahead)
At the **next mini-roundabout (5)** take the **1st** exit (straight ahead)
At the traffic lights continue straight ahead into **STIFFORD HILL**
Then take the **1st** turning on the left continuing along **STIFFORD HILL**
Continue into **HIGH ROAD**
At the **next roundabout (6)** take the **4th** exit on to the **A13** LONDON
Once on the **A13** leave at the **1st** slip-road
This leads to the **next roundabout (7)** which is Junction **30** of the **M25**
Follow the signs for the direction you wish to travel

Route 2 **Roundabouts (6)**

Leave the **M25** at Junction **29** follow the slip-road
At the **1st roundabout** take the **3rd** exit on to the **SOUTHEND ARTERIAL ROAD (A127)**
Take the **3rd** turning on the left and at the **T** Junction turn left into **HALL LANE**
At the **next roundabout (2)** take the **2nd** exit (straight ahead)
Continue into **STATION ROAD**
At the Major traffic lights continue into **CORBETS TAY ROAD**
At the left hand bend turn right into **HARWOOD HALL LANE** following the signs for AVELEY
At the **next roundabout (3)** take the **1st** exit (turn left) into **AVELEY ROAD**
Continue into **ROMFORD ROAD**
At the **next roundabout (4)** take the **3rd** exit into **SANDY LANE (B1335)**
At the **T** junction turn left into **NEW ROAD**
At the **next roundabout (5)** take the **1st** exit on to **A13**
Once on the **A13** leave at the **1st** slip-road
This leads to the **next roundabout (6)** which is Junction **30** of the **M25**
Follow the signs for the direction you wish to travel

<u>JUNCTIONS 30 - 31 (CLOCKWISE)</u>

<u>Route 1</u> **<u>Roundabouts (2)</u>**

Leave the **M25** at Junction **30** follow the slip-road
At the **1st roundabout** take the **2nd** exit on to the **A13** following the signs for **<u>THURROCK SERVICES</u>**
Keep on the slip-road and continue past the **<u>SERVICES</u>**
This leads to the **next roundabout (2)** which is Junction **31** of the **M25**
<u>Follow the signs for the direction you wish to travel</u>

<u>Route 2</u> **<u>Roundabouts (3)</u>**

Leave the **M25** at Junction **30** follow the slip-road
At the **1st roundabout** take the **3rd** exit on to the **A13** following the signs for **<u>LONDON E+C</u>**
Once on the **A13** leave at the **1st** slip-road
At the **next roundabout (2)** take the **1st** exit (turn left) on to **LONDON ROAD**
Continue into **ARTERIAL ROAD PURFLEET**
This leads to the **next roundabout (3)** which is Junction **31** of the **M25**
<u>Follow the signs for the direction you wish to travel</u>

<u>JUNCTIONS 31 - 30 (ANTI-CLOCKWISE)</u>

<u>**Route 1**</u> <u>**Roundabouts (4)**</u>

Exit the <u>**DARTFORD TUNNEL**</u> into **CANTERBURY WAY (A282)**
Leave at the **1st** slip-road and keep to the left hand lane
At the **1st roundabout** take the **2nd** exit into **ARTERIAL ROAD PURFLEET**
Continue into **LONDON ROAD**
At the **next roundabout (2)** take the **2nd** exit (straight ahead)
At the **next roundabout (3)** take the **2nd** exit (turn right) on to the **A13** following the signs for **M25**
Once on the **A13** leave at the **1st** slip-road
This leads to the **next roundabout (4)** which is Junction **30** of the **M25**
<u>**Follow the signs for the direction you wish to travel**</u>

<u>**Route 2**</u> <u>**Roundabouts (7)**</u>

Exit the <u>**DARTFORD TUNNEL**</u> into the **CANTERBURY WAY (A282)**
Leave at the **1st** slip-road and keep to the left hand lane
At the **1st roundabout** take the **5th** exit into **ARTERIAL ROAD WEST THURROCK (A1306)**
At the **next roundabout (2)** take the **3rd** exit (straight ahead)
At the **next roundabout (3)** take the **3rd** exit (straight ahead)
At the **next roundabout (4)** take the **2nd** exit (straight ahead) into the **ARTERIAL ROAD NORTH STIFFORD (A1306)**
At the **next roundabout (5)** take the **1st** exit into **ELIZABETH ROAD (A1012)**
At the **next roundabout (6)** take the **1st** exit (turn left) on to the **A13** following the signs for **M25** <u>**DARTFORD TUNNEL**</u>
Once on the **A13** leave at the **1st** slip-road
This leads to the **next roundabout (7)** which is Junction **30** of the **M25**
<u>**Follow the signs for the direction you wish to travel**</u>

<u>**Route 3**</u> <u>**Roundabouts (2)**</u>

Exit the <u>**DARTFORD TUNNEL**</u> into the **CANTERBURY WAY (A282)**
Leave at the **1st** slip-road and keep to the left hand lane
At the **1st roundabout** take the **4th** exit on to the **A13**
Keep left following the signs for the **M25** <u>**NORTH**</u>
This leads to the **next roundabout (2)** which is Junction **30** of the **M25**
<u>**Follow the signs for the direction you wish to travel**</u>

JUNCTIONS 30 - 29 (ANTI-CLOCKWISE)

Route 1 **Roundabouts (7)**

Leave the **M25** at Junction **30** follow the slip-road
At the **1st roundabout** take the **3rd** exit on to the **A13** following the signs for **THURROCK**
Once on the **A13** leave at the **2nd** slip-road
At the **next roundabout (2)** take the **1st** exit (turn left) into **HIGH ROAD**
Continue into **STIFFORD HILL**
At the **T** Junction turn right continuing along **STIFFORD HILL (B186)**
At the traffic lights continue straight ahead into **SOUTH ROAD (B186)**
At the **1st mini-roundabout (3)** take the **2nd** exit (straight ahead)
At the **next mini-roundabout (4)** take the **2nd** exit (straight ahead)
At the **next mini-roundabout (5)** take the **1st** exit (straight ahead)
Continue into **NORTH ROAD** Continue into **OCKENDON ROAD**
Continue into **CLAY TYE ROAD (B186)**
At the **next mini-roundabout (6)** take the **2nd** exit into **ST MARY'S LANE**
Continue into **WARLEY STREET (B186)**
Take the **3rd** turning on the right into **SOUTHEND ARTERIAL ROAD (A127)** following the signs for **LONDON M25** and leave at the **1st** slip-road
This leads to the **next roundabout (7)** which is Junction **29** of the **M25**
Follow the signs for the direction you wish to travel

Route 2 **Roundabouts (7)**

Leave the **M25** at Junction **30** follow the slip-road
At the **1st roundabout** take the **1st** exit on to the **A13** follow signs for **LONDON**
Once on the **A13** leave at the **1st** slip-road
At the **next roundabout (2)** take the **3rd** exit (turn right)
At the **next roundabout (3)** take the **1st** exit (straight ahead) into **NEW ROAD**
Then take the **1st** turning on the right into **SANDY LANE (B1335)**
At the **next roundabout (4)** take the **1st** exit (turn left) into **ROMFORD ROAD**
Continue into **AVELEY ROAD**
At the **1st mini-roundabout (5)** take the **2nd** exit into **HARWOOD HALL LANE**
At the Junction turn left into **CORBETS TEY ROAD**
Continue into **STATION ROAD** Continue into **HALL LANE**
At the **mini-roundabout (6)** take the **1st** exit (straight ahead)
Keep left and follow the slip-road on to **SOUTHEND ARTERIAL ROAD (A127)**
Leave at the **1st** slip-road following the signs for the **M25**
This leads to the **next roundabout (7)** which is Junction **29** of the **M25**
Follow the signs for the direction you wish to travel

JUNCTIONS 29 - 28 (ANTI-CLOCKWISE)

Route 1 **Roundabouts (2)**

Leave the **M25** at Junction **29** follow the slip-road
At the **1st roundabout** take **1st** exit (turn left) into the **SOUTHEND ARTERIAL ROAD (A127)**
Once on the **A13** take the **3rd** turning on the left
At the **T** Junction turn right and cross over the **(A127)**
Then take the **1st** turning on the right into **HALL LANE**
At the **T** Junction turn right then immediate left into **NAGS HEAD LANE**
At the traffic lights turn left into **BROOK STREET (A1023)**
This leads to the **next roundabout (2)** which is Junction **28** of the **M25**
Follow the signs for the direction you wish to travel

Route 2 **Roundabouts (2)**

Leave the **M25** at Junction **29** follow the slip-road
At the **1st roundabout** take the **3rd** exit (turn right) on to the **SOUTHEND ARTERIAL ROAD (A127)** following the signs for **SOUTHEND**
As you join the **SOUTHEND ARTERIAL ROAD** leave at the **1st** slip-road
At the **T** Junction turn left into **WARLEY STREET (B186)**
Continue into **GREAT WARLEY STREET (B186)**
Continue into **WARLEY ROAD**
At the traffic lights turn left into **MASCALLS LANE**
At the next set of traffic lights turn left into **BROOK STREET (A1023)**
This leads to the **next roundabout (2)** which is Junction **28** of the **M25**
Follow the signs for the direction you wish to travel

JUNCTIONS 28 - 27 (ANTI-CLOCKWISE)

Route 1 **Roundabouts (4)**

Leave the **M25** at Junction **28** follow the slip-road
At the **1st roundabout** take the **1st** exit (turn left) into **COLCHESTER ROAD (A12)**
At the **next roundabout (2)** take the **3rd** exit into **EASTERN AVENUE EAST (A12)** following the signs for **LONDON**
Follow for about 7 miles via **EASTERN AVENUE WEST (A12)**
Continuing into **EASTERN AVENUE (A12)**
At the **next roundabout (3)** take the **3rd** exit continuing along **EASTERN AVENUE (A12)** following the signs for the **M11**
At the **next roundabout (4)** take the **4th** exit (turn right)
Keep to the left hand lane following the signs for **STANSTED (M11)**
Once on the **M11** leave at the **2nd** slip-road following the signs for the **M25**
This leads to Junction **27** of the **M25**
Follow the signs for the direction you wish to travel

Route 2 **Roundabouts (6)**

Leave the **M25** at Junction **28** follow the slip-road
At the **1st roundabout** take the **4th** exit into **BROOK STREET (A1023)**
At the **1st** set of traffic lights turn left into **WIGLEY BUSH LANE**
At the **T** Junction turn left into **WEALD ROAD**
Then take the **1st** turning on the right into **LINCOLNS LANE**
At the **T** Junction turn left then immediate right into **MORES LANE**
At the **next T** Junction turn left into **ONGAR ROAD (A128)**
Continue into **BRENTWOOD ROAD (A128)**
At the **1st mini-roundabout (2)** take the **3rd** exit (turn right) into **COOPER'S HILL**
Continue into **HIGH STREET**
At the **next roundabout (3)** take the **1st** exit (turn left) into **EPPING ROAD (A414)**
At the **next roundabout (4)** take the **2nd** exit (straight ahead)
At the **next roundabout (5)** take the **2nd** exit into **CANES LANE**
At the **next roundabout (6)** take the **1st** exit on to the **M11** following the signs for **M25 LONDON**
Once on the **M11** leave at the **1st** slip-road
This leads to Junction **27** of the **M25**
Follow the signs for the direction you wish to travel

JUNCTIONS 27 - 26 (ANTI-CLOCKWISE)

Route 1 **Roundabouts (4)**

Leave the **M25** at Junction **27** follow the slip-road
Keep to the left following the signs for the **M11** **LONDON**
Once on the **M11** leave at the **1st** slip-road which is Junction **4** of the **M11**
Keep in right hand lane following the signs for **WALTHAMSTOW (A406)**
This leads on to the **SOUTHEND ROAD (A406)**
Keep in the left hand lane
Leave at the **1st** slip-road following the signs for **WOODFORD (A104)**
At the **1st roundabout** take the **3rd** exit into **WOODFORD NEW ROAD (A104)**
At the T Junction continue straight ahead into **HIGH ROAD (A11)**
Continue into **WOODFORD GREEN**
Continue into **EPPING NEW ROAD (A104)**
At the **next roundabout (2)** take the **2nd** exit (straight ahead)
At the **next roundabout (3)** take the **1st** exit into **WOODRIDDEN HILL (A121)**
Continue into **HONEY LANE**
This leads to the **next roundabout (4)** which is Junction **26** of the **M25**
Follow the signs for the direction you wish to travel

Route 2 **Roundabouts (5)**

Leave the **M25** at Junction **27** follow the slip-road
Keep to the right following the signs for **M11** **CAMBRIDGE**
Once on the **M11** leave at the **1st** slip-road which is Junction 7 of the **M11**
At the **1st roundabout** take the **1st** exit (turn left) into **LONDON ROAD (B1393)**
Continue into **HIGH ROAD**
Continue into **THORNWOOD ROAD**
Continue into **PALMERS HILL**
At the **1st mini-roundabout (2)** take the **1st** exit (straight ahead)
At the **next mini-roundabout (3)** take the **2nd** exit (straight ahead)
Continue into **HIGH STREET**
Continue into **HIGH ROAD**
Continue into **EPPING ROAD**
At the **next roundabout (4)** take the **4th** exit (turn right) into **WOODRIDDEN HILL (A121)**
Continue into **HONEY LANE**
This leads to the **next roundabout (5)** which is Junction **26** of the **M25**
Follow the signs for the direction you wish to travel

<u>JUNCTIONS 26 - 25 (ANTI-CLOCKWISE)</u>

<u>Route 1</u> **<u>Roundabouts (7)</u>**

Leave the **M25** at Junction **26** follow the slip-road
At the **1st roundabout** take the **2nd** exit following the signs for **<u>WALTHAM CROSS</u>**
At the **next roundabout (2)** take the **2nd** exit (straight ahead) following the signs for **A121**
At the **next roundabout (3)** take the **2nd** exit (straight ahead)
At the traffic lights turn left into **STATION ROAD (A121)**
Continue into **ELEANOR CROSS ROAD (A121)**
At the **next roundabout (4)** take the **3rd** exit into **MONARCHS WAY**
Continue into **HIGH STREET (A121)**
At the **next roundabout (5)** take **2nd** exit into **WINSTON CHURCHILL WAY** following the signs for the **M25**
At the **next roundabout (6)** take the **1st** exit (turn left) into the **GREAT CAMBRIDGE ROAD (A10)**
This leads to the **next roundabout (7)** which is Junction **25** of the **M25**
<u>Follow the signs for the direction you wish to travel</u>

<u>Route 2</u> **<u>Roundabouts (5)</u>**

Leave the **M25** at Junction **26** follow the slip-road
At the **1st roundabout** take the **2nd** exit following the signs for **<u>WALTHAM CROSS</u>**
At the **next roundabout (2)** take the **1st** exit (turn left) into **SEWARDSTONE ROAD (A112)**
At the traffic lights turn right into **LEA VALLEY ROAD (A110)**
At the **next roundabout (2)** take the **3rd** exit (turn right) into **MOLLISON AVENUE (A1055)**
At the **next roundabout (3)** take the **2nd** exit (straight ahead)
At the **next roundabout (4)** take the **1st** exit (straight ahead)
Continue into **BULLSMOOR LANE**
Following the signs for the **M25** turn right into **GREAT CAMBRIDGE ROAD (A10)**
This leads to the **next roundabout (5)** which is Junction **25** of the **M25**
<u>Follow the signs for the direction you wish to travel</u>

JUNCTIONS 25 - 24 (ANTI-CLOCKWISE)

Route 1 **Roundabouts (2)**

Leave the **M25** at Junction **25** follow the slip-road
At the **1st roundabout** take the **1st** exit into **GREAT CAMBRIDGE ROAD (A10)** and keep in the right hand lane
At the **1st** set of traffic lights turn right into **BULLSMOOR LANE**
Then take the **1st** turning on the right into **BULL'S CROSS**
Continue left into **WHITEWEBBS LANE**
Continue into **WHITEWEBBS ROAD**
At the **T** Junction turn right into **THEOBALDS PARK ROAD**
Continue left into **CATTLEGATE ROAD** continue under the railway bridge
Then take the **1st** turning on the left into **EAST LODGE LANE**
At the **T** Junction turn right into **THE RIDGEWAY (A1005)**
This leads to the **next roundabout (2)** which is Junction **24** of the **M25**
Follow the signs for the direction you wish to travel

Route 2 **Roundabouts (9)**

Leave the **M25** at Junction **25** follow the slip-road
At the **1st roundabout** take the **3rd** exit (turn right) into **GREAT CAMBRIDGE ROAD (A10)**
At the **next roundabout (2)** take the **1st** exit into **LIEUTENANT ELLIS WAY**
At the **next roundabout (3)** take the **1st** exit into **GOFF'S LANE (B156)**
At the **next roundabout (4)** take the **1st** exit (straight ahead) into **CUFFLEY HILL (B156)**
At the **1st mini roundabout (5)** take the **1st** exit (straight ahead) into **STATION ROAD**
At the **T** Junction turn left into **NORTHAW ROAD EAST (B156)**
At the **mini-roundabout (6)** take the **1st** exit (straight ahead)
Continue into **NORTHAW ROAD WEST**
At the **mini-roundabout (7)** take the **1st** exit (straight ahead)
At the **mini-roundabout (8)** take the **1st** exit (straight ahead) into **JUDGE'S HILL**
Continue into **COOPER'S LANE**
Continue into **THE CAUSEWAY**
At the traffic lights continue straight ahead into **HIGH STREET (A1000)**
At the main set of traffic lights turn left into **SOUTHGATE ROAD (A111)** following the signs for **M25**
This leads to the **next roundabout (9)** which is Junction **24** of the **M25**
Follow the signs for the direction you wish to travel

JUNCTIONS 24 - 23 (ANTI-CLOCKWISE)

Route 1 **Roundabouts (6)**

Leave the **M25** at Junction **24** follow the slip-road
At the **1st roundabout** take the **4th** exit into **SOUTHGATE ROAD (A111)**
At the traffic lights continue straight ahead into **MUTTON LANE (B556)**
At the **1st mini-roundabout (2)** take the **1st** exit (straight ahead)
Continue into **CECIL ROAD** following the signs for **SOUTH MIMMS SERVICES**
At the **next roundabout (3)** take the **1st** exit (turn left) into **ST ALBANS ROAD**
At the **next roundabout (4)** take the **2nd** exit into **ST ALBANS ROAD**
At the **next roundabout (5)** which is **BIGNELL'S CORNER** follow the signs for **M25**
This leads to the **next roundabout (6)** which is Junction **23** of the **M25**
Follow the signs for the direction you wish to travel

Route 2 **Roundabouts (2)**

Leave the **M25** at Junction **24** follow the slip-road
At the **1st roundabout** take the **2nd** exit into **COCKFOSTERS ROAD**
Continue into **STAGG HILL (A111)**
Take the **1st** turning on the right into **WAGGON ROAD**
Continue into **WAGON ROAD**
At the crossroads (main road) continue straight ahead continuing into **WAGON ROAD**
At the **T** Junction turn left into **DANCERS HILL ROAD**
At the next **T** Junction turn right into **ST ALBANS ROAD (A1081)**
This leads to the **next roundabout (2)** which is Junction **23** of the **M25**
Follow the signs for the direction you wish to travel

JUNCTIONS 23 - 22 (ANTI-CLOCKWISE)

Route 1 **Roundabouts (5)**

Leave the **M25** at Junction **23** follow the slip-road
At the **1st roundabout** take the **5th** exit into the **SOUTH MIMMS SERVICES**
Keep to the left
Then take the **1st** turning on the left into **SWANLAND ROAD** following the signs for **SOUTH MIMMS**
At the **next roundabout (2)** take the **1st** exit into **ST ALBANS ROAD (B556)**
At the **next roundabout (3)** take the **1st** exit (straight ahead) continuing along **ST ALBANS ROAD (B556)**
At the **next roundabout (4)** take the **1st** exit (straight ahead) into **BELL LANE**
This leads to the **next roundabout (5)** which is Junction **22** of the **M25**
Follow the signs for the direction you wish to travel

Route 2 **Roundabouts (6)**

Leave the **M25** at Junction **23** follow the slip-road
At the **1st roundabout** take the **5th** exit towards the **SOUTH MIMMS SERVICES** into **BIGNELL'S CORNER**
Keep to the left
Then take the **1st** left into **SWANLAND ROAD** following the signs for **COLNEY HEATH**
At the **next roundabout (2)** take the **2nd** exit (straight ahead) continuing along **SWANLAND ROAD**
At the **T** Junction turn left into **TOLLGATE ROAD** following the signs for **COLNEY HEATH**
At the **next roundabout (3)** take the **1st** exit (turn left) into **COURSERS ROAD**
At the **next roundabout (4)** take the **2nd** exit into **BELL LANE (A1081)** continuing over the **M25**
At the **next roundabout (5)** take the **2nd** exit continuing along **BELL LANE**
This leads to the **next roundabout (6)** which is Junction **22** of the **M25**
Follow the signs for the direction you wish to travel

<u>JUNCTIONS 22 - 21a (ANTI-CLOCKWISE)</u>

You cannot leave the M25 for the M1 North if you join the M25 at Junction 21a, you will have to follow the North Orbital Road (A405) at Junction 21a following the signs for the M1 North this will lead to Junction 6 of the M1

<u>**Route 1**</u> <u>**Roundabouts (7)**</u>

Leave the **M25** at Junction **22** follow the slip-road
At the **1st roundabout** take the **3rd** exit (turn right) continuing over the **M25**
At the **next roundabout (2)** take the **3rd** exit on to the **LONDON COLNEY BY-PASS (A1081)**
At the **next roundabout (3)** take the **2nd** exit into **NORTH ORBITAL ROAD (A414)**
At the **next roundabout (4)** take the **2nd** exit continuing along **NORTH ORBITAL ROAD (A405)**
At the **next roundabout (5)** take the **2nd** exit (straight ahead)
At the **next roundabout (6)** take the **1st** exit (straight ahead)
This leads to the **next roundabout (7)** which is Junction **21a** of the **M25**
<u>**Follow the signs for the direction you wish to travel**</u>

<u>**Route 2**</u> <u>**Roundabouts (4)**</u>

Leave the **M25** at Junction **22** follow the slip-road
At the **1st roundabout** take the **2nd** exit (straight ahead) into **BELL LANE (B556)**
At the **next roundabout (2)** take the **1st** exit continuing along **BELL LANE**
At the **next roundabout (3)** take the **2nd** exit (straight ahead) into **HARPER LANE**
At the **T** Junction turn right into **RADLETT ROAD (B5183)**
Take the **1st** turning on the left into **SMUG OAK LANE**
At the **T** Junction turn right into **STATION ROAD**
As you pass over the bridge turn left into **LYE LANE**
Take the **1st** turning on the right continuing along **LYE LANE**
At the **T** Junction turn left on to the **NORTH ORBITAL ROAD (A405)**
This leads to the **next roundabout (4)** which is Junction **21a** of the **M25**
<u>**Follow the signs for the direction you wish to travel**</u>

JUNCTIONS 21a - 21 (ANTI-CLOCKWISE)

Route 1 is only worth taking if you are heading on to the M1 northbound stay on once you are on the M1 instead of leaving at Junction 8 of the M1
If you need to join the M1 southbound leave the M25 at Junction 21a following the NORTH ORBITAL ROAD (A405) this leads to Junction 6 of the M1

Route 1 **Roundabouts (5)**

Leave the **M25** at Junction **21a** follow the slip-road
At the **1st roundabout** take the **3rd** exit into **NORTH ORBITAL ROAD (A405)**
At the **next roundabout (2)** take the **2nd** exit (ignore the hotel entrance) continuing along **NORTH ORBITAL ROAD (A405)**
At the **next roundabout (3)** take the **2nd** exit (straight ahead)
At the **next roundabout (4)** take the **1st** exit (turn left) on to the **M10**
Leave at the **1st** slip-road which is Junction **8** on the **M1** following the signs for **HEMEL HEMPSTEAD** and keep left into **BREAKSPEAR WAY (A414)**
At the **next roundabout (5)** take the **4th** exit (U-turn)
This leads to Junction **8** of the **M1** continue straight ahead following the signs for the **M1 SOUTH**
Once on the **M1 SOUTHBOUND** leave at the **2nd** slip-road
This leads to Junction **21** and the **M25 WESTBOUND**
Follow the signs for the direction you wish to travel

JUNCTIONS 21a - 20 (ANTI-CLOCKWISE)

Route 1 **Roundabouts (6)**

Leave the **M25** at Junction **21a** follow the slip-road
At the **1st roundabout** take the **1st** exit into **NORTH ORBITAL ROAD (A405)**
Keep in the right hand lane turn **1st** right then turn right again completing a **U-Turn** back into **NORTH ORBITAL ROAD (A405)**
Then take the **1st** turning on the left into **CHEQUERS LANE**
Bear left into **WOODSIDE ROAD**
At the **1st mini-roundabout (2)** take the **2nd** exit (turn right) into **COLLEGE ROAD**
At the **next roundabout (3)** take the **2nd** exit (straight ahead)
At the **next roundabout (4)** take the **1st** exit (turn left) into **LANGLEY LANE**
At the **next roundabout (5)** take the **3rd** exit (turn right) into **SOUTH WAY**
Continue into **HUNTON BRIDGE HILL** Continue **BRIDGE ROAD**
At the traffic lights turn right into **WATFORD ROAD (A41)** follow signs for **M25**
This leads to the **next roundabout (6)** which is Junction **20** of the **M25**
Follow the signs for the direction you wish to travel

JUNCTIONS 21 - 20 (ANTI-CLOCKWISE)

Route 1 **Roundabouts (9)**

Leave the **M25** at Junction **21** follow the **1st** slip-road on to the **M1** **NORTHBOUND**

Once on the **M1** leave at the **1st** slip-road which is Junction **8** of the **M1**

Follow the slip-road into **BREAKSPEAR WAY (A414)**

At the **1st roundabout** take the **2nd** exit (straight ahead)

At the **next roundabout (2)** take the **2nd** exit (straight ahead) into **ST ALBANS ROAD (A414)**

At the **next roundabout (3)** take the **2nd** exit (straight ahead)

At the **next roundabout (4)** take the **2nd** exit continuing along **ST ALBANS ROAD (A414)**

At the **1st mini-roundabout (5)** take the **1st** exit (turn left)

At the **next mini-roundabout (6)** take the **2nd** exit (straight ahead)

At the **next mini-roundabout (7)** take the **1st** exit (turn left) into **TWO WATERS ROAD**

At the **next roundabout (8)** take the **1st** exit (turn left) on to the **A41** following the signs for the **M25**

This leads to the **next roundabout (9)** which is Junction **20** of the **M25**

Follow the signs for the direction you wish to travel

JUNCTIONS 20 - 19 (ANTI-CLOCKWISE)

You should only need to use this route if the M25 is blocked between Junctions 20-19 as you cannot leave the M25 at Junction 19

Route 1 **Roundabouts (2)**

Leave the **M25** at Junction **20** follow the slip-road
At the **1st roundabout** take the **1st** exit (turn left) into **WATFORD ROAD (A41)**
At the **next roundabout (2)** take the **3rd** exit (turn right) on to the **M25**
This leads on to the **M25** at Junction **19**
Follow the signs for the direction you wish to travel

JUNCTIONS 20 - 18 (ANTI-CLOCKWISE)

Route 1 **Roundabouts (8)**

Leave the **M25** at Junction **20** follow the slip-road
At the **1st roundabout** take the **1st** exit into **WATFORD ROAD (A41)**
At the **next roundabout (2)** take the **2nd** exit (straight ahead) into **HEMPSTEAD ROAD (A411)**
This leads to the one way system at **WATFORD**
Follow the one way system
At the **next roundabout (3)** take the **3rd** exit (turn right) into **RICKMANSWORTH ROAD (A412)**
At the **next roundabout (4)** take the **2nd** exit (straight ahead)
At the **next roundabout (5)** take the **1st** exit (straight ahead) into **WATFORD ROAD (A412)**
At the **next roundabout (6)** take the **1st** exit (straight ahead) into **SCOTS HILL**
Continue into **PARK ROAD**
At the **next roundabout (7)** take the **2nd** exit (straight ahead)
At the **next roundabout (8)** take the **2nd** exit (turn right) into **CHORLEYWOOD ROAD (A404)**
This leads to Junction **18** of the **M25**
Follow the signs for the direction you wish to travel

JUNCTIONS 18 - 17 (ANTI-CLOCKWISE)

Route 1 **Roundabouts (4)**

Leave the **M25** at Junction **18** follow the slip-road
At the traffic lights turn left into **CHORLEYWOOD ROAD (A404)**
At the **1st roundabout** take the **2nd** exit (turn right) into **RECTORY ROAD**
At the **next roundabout (2)** take the **3rd** exit (turn right) into **UXBRIDGE ROAD (A412)**
At the **next roundabout (3)** take the **2nd** exit (turn right) into **DENHAM WAY (A412)** following the signs for the **M25**
This leads to the **next roundabout (4)** which is Junction **17** of the **M25**
Follow the signs for the direction you wish to travel

Route 2 **Roundabouts (1)**

Leave the **M25** at Junction **18** follow the slip-road
At the traffic lights turn right into **RICKMANSWORTH ROAD (A404)**
At the **2nd** set of traffic lights turn left into **DOG KENNEL LANE**
At the **T** Junction turn right into **BERRY LANE**
Continue into **STAG LANE**
At the next **T** Junction turn left into **LONG LANE**
This leads to the **1st roundabout** which is Junction **17** of the **M25**
Follow the signs for the direction you wish to travel

JUNCTIONS 17 - 16 (ANTI-CLOCKWISE)

Route 1 **Roundabouts (4)**

Leave the **M25** at Junction **17** follow the slip-road
At the **1st roundabout** take the **1st** exit into **DENHAM WAY (A412)**
At the **next roundabout (2)** take the **2nd** exit (turn right) continuing along **DENHAM WAY (A412)**
At the **next roundabout (3)** take the **2nd** exit (straight ahead)
Continue into **DENHAM AVENUE**
At the traffic lights at the **A40** turn left into **OXFORD ROAD (A40)**
Keep in the right hand lane
At the **1st mini-roundabout (4)** turn right
Keep right then at the **2nd** set of traffic lights turn right on to the **M40** following the signs for **OXFORD M40**
Once on the **M40** leave at the **1st** slip-road
This leads to Junction **16** of the **M25**
Follow the signs for the direction you wish to travel

Route 2 **Roundabouts (5)**

Leave the **M25** at Junction **17** follow the slip-road
At the **1st roundabout** take the **3rd** exit (turn right) into **LONG LANE**
Continue into **HERONSGATE ROAD**
Take the **4th** turning on the left into **CHALFONT LANE** following the signs for **LITTLE CHALFONT**
At the crossroads turn left into **BURTONS LANE**
Take the **1st** turning on the left into **ROUGHWOOD LANE**
At the T Junction turn left into **NIGHTINGALES LANE (B4442)**
At the **1st mini roundabout (2)** take the **1st** exit (turn left) into **AMERSHAM ROAD (A413)**
At the **next roundabout (3)** take the **2nd** exit (straight ahead) into **CHALFONT ST PETER BY-PASS (A413)**
At the **next roundabout (4)** take the **2nd** exit (straight ahead)
Continue into **AMERSHAM ROAD**
Keep left into **OXFORD ROAD (A40)**
Keep in the right hand lane
At the **mini-roundabout (5)** turn right keep to the right hand lane
At the **2nd** set of traffic lights turn right on to the **M40** follow signs for **OXFORD**
Once on the **M40** leave at the **1st** slip-road
This leads to Junction **16** of the **M25**
Follow the signs for the direction you wish to travel

<u>JUNCTIONS 16 - 15 (ANTI-CLOCKWISE)</u>

<u>Route 1</u> **<u>Roundabouts (9)</u>**

Leave the **M25** at Junction **16** follow the slip-road and keep left on to the **M40** following the signs for **<u>LONDON</u>**
Once on the **M40** leave at the **1st** slip-road
At the traffic lights turn right then keep left
At the **1st roundabout** take the **1st** exit (straight ahead)
At the **next roundabout (2)** take **2nd** exit into **OXFORD ROAD (A4020)** following the signs for **<u>UXBRIDGE</u>**
At the **next roundabout (3)** take the **3rd** exit into **COWLEY ROAD (A408)**
At the **next roundabout (4)** take the **4th** exit into **COWLEY ROAD** following the signs to **<u>COWLEY</u> (A408)**
Continue into the **HIGH STREET**
At the **next roundabout (5)** take the **1st** exit (straight ahead)
Continue into **HIGH ROAD** Continue into **HIGH STREET**
Keep left at the traffic lights into **FALLING LANE** following the signs for the **M4**
At the **next roundabout (6)** take the **2nd** exit into **PARK VIEW ROAD**
At the **next roundabout (7)** take the **2nd** exit into **STOCKLEY ROAD**
At the **next roundabout (8)** take the **2nd** exit (straight ahead) and keep to the right
At the major crossroads continue straight ahead following the signs for **<u>SLOUGH</u>**
At the **next roundabout (9)** take the **3rd** exit on to the **M4**
Once on the **M4** leave at the **1st** slip-road
This leads to Junction **15** of the **M25**
<u>Follow the signs for the direction you wish to travel.</u>

<u>Route 2</u> **<u>Roundabouts (6)</u>**

Leave the **M25** at Junction **16** keep left on to the **M40** follow signs for **<u>LONDON</u>**
Once on the **M40** leave at the **1st** slip-road
At the traffic lights turn right then keep to the left
At the **1st roundabout** take the **2nd** exit (turn right) into **DENHAM ROAD (A412)**
At the **next roundabout (2)** take the **2nd** exit (straight ahead)
At the **mini-roundabout (3)** take the **1st** exit (straight on) into **CHURCH ROAD**
At the **next roundabout (4)** take the **3rd** exit into **UXBRIDGE ROAD (A412)**
At the **next roundabout (5)** take the **1st** exit (turn left) into **SUSSEX PLACE**
Continue into **LONDON ROAD (A4)** following the signs for **M4**
At the **next roundabout (6)** take the **1st** exit on to the **M4** **<u>LONDON</u>**
Once on the **M4** leave at the **1st** slip-road
This leads to Junction **15** of the **M25**
<u>Follow the signs for the direction you wish to travel</u>

JUNCTIONS 15 - 14 (ANTI-CLOCKWISE)

Route 1 **Roundabouts (7)**

Leave the **M25** at Junction **15** follow the slip-road
Keep to the left following the signs for the **M4** **CENTRAL LONDON**
Once on the **M4** leave at the **1st** slip-road
At **1st roundabout** take the **1st** exit following signs for **HARMONDSWORTH**
Turn immediate left and at the filter lane before the traffic lights turn left again into **HOLLOWAY LANE (A3044)**
At the **next roundabout (2)** take the **2nd** exit (straight ahead)
At the **mini-roundabout (3)** take **1st** exit continuing along **HOLLOWAY LANE**
At the **next roundabout (4)** take the **1st** exit into **HATCH LANE**
At the traffic lights turn right into **COLNBROOK BY-PASS (A4)**
At the main traffic lights turn left into **STANWELL MOOR ROAD (A3044)**
At the **next roundabout (5)** take the **2nd** exit (straight ahead)
At the **next roundabout (6)** take the **3rd** exit into **AIRPORT WAY (A3113)**
This leads to the **next roundabout (7)** which is Junction **14** of the **M25**
Follow the signs for the direction you wish to travel

Route 2 **Roundabouts (3)**

Leave the **M25** at Junction **15** follow the slip-road
Then keep in the right-hand slip-road following the signs for the **M4** **SLOUGH**
Once on the **M4** leave at the **1st** slip-road
At the **1st roundabout** take the **1st** exit into **LONDON ROAD (A4)** following the signs for **STAINES**
Keep in the right hand lane following the signs to **COLNBROOK** turning right then immediate left into **LONDON ROAD** (off of the **A4)**
Continue into **HIGH STREET** following the hairpin bend to the right into **HORTON ROAD**
At the **T** Junction turn left into **STANWELL ROAD**
Continue into **HORTON ROAD**
At the **next roundabout (2)** take the **2nd** exit (straight ahead)
This leads to the **next roundabout (3)** which is Junction **14** of the **M25**
Follow the signs for the direction you wish to travel

JUNCTIONS 14 - 13 (ANTI-CLOCKWISE)

Route 1 **Roundabouts (4)**

Leave the **M25** at Junction **14** follow the slip-road
At the **1st roundabout** take the **1st** exit into **AIRPORT WAY (A3113)**
At the **next roundabout (2)** take the **3rd** exit (turn right) into **STANWELL MOOR ROAD (A3044)**
At the **2nd** set of traffic lights keep in the right hand lane following the signs for the **M25**
At the **3rd** set of traffic lights (30yds) turn right into **STAINES BY-PASS (A30)** following the signs for the **M25**
This leads to the **next roundabout (4)** which is Junction **13** of the **M25**
Follow the signs for the direction you wish to travel

Route 2 **Roundabouts (4)**

Leave the **M25** at Junction **14** follow the slip-road
At the **1st roundabout** take the **4th** exit into **HORTON ROAD** following the signs for **POYLE**
At the **next roundabout (2)** take the **1st** exit (straight ahead) continuing along **HORTON ROAD**
Continue into **STANWELL ROAD**
Then take the **1st** turning on the left into **COPPERMILL ROAD**
Continue into **STATION ROAD**
Continue into **HIGH STREET**
Continue into **STAINES ROAD (B376)**
Continue into **WRAYSBURY ROAD**
At the **next roundabout (3)** take the **1st** exit (turn left)
This leads to the **next roundabout (4)** which is Junction **13** of the **M25**
Follow the signs for the direction you wish to travel

JUNCTIONS 13 - 12 (ANTI-CLOCKWISE)

Route 1 **Roundabouts (4)**

Leave the **M25** at Junction **13** follow the slip-road
At the **1st roundabout** take the **1st** exit on to the **STAINES BY-PASS (A30)**
At the **next roundabout (2)** keep left follow the signs **KINGSTON (A308)** turning right (across the **A30**) into **STAINES BY-PASS (A308)**
At the **next roundabout (3)** take the **2nd** exit (straight ahead) into **KINGSTON ROAD (A308)**
Continue into **STAINES ROAD WEST**
At the **next roundabout (4)** take the **5th** exit on to the **M3** following the signs for **PORTSMOUTH (M3)**
Once on the **M3** leave at the **1st** slip-road
This will lead into Junction **12** of the **M25**
Follow the signs for the direction you wish to travel

Route 2 **Roundabouts (4)**

Leave the **M25** at Junction **13** follow the slip-road
At the **1st roundabout** take the **2nd** exit (straight ahead)
Keep to the left hand lane following the signs for **EGHAM**
At the **next roundabout (2)** take the **2nd** exit into **EGHAM BY-PASS (A30)**
At the **next roundabout (3)** take the **3rd** exit (straight ahead) into **EGHAM HILL (A30)** following the signs for **BASINGSTOKE**
Continue into **LONDON ROAD** for about **5** miles
At the **next roundabout (4)** take the **1st** exit (turn left) into **GROVE END**
At the **T** Junction turn left into **BRACKNELL ROAD (A322)**
This leads to the **next roundabout (4)** which is Junction **3** of the **M3**
Then take the **1st** exit (turn left) on to the **M3** following the signs for **LONDON**
Once on the **M3** leave at the **1st** slip-road
This leads into Junction **12** of the **M25**
Follow the signs for the direction you wish to travel

JUNCTIONS 12 - 11 (ANTI-CLOCKWISE)

Route 1 **Roundabouts (6)**

Leave the **M25** at Junction **12** follow the slip-road
Then keep in the right hand slip-road and the signs for **M3 PORTSMOUTH**
Once on the **M3** leave at the **1st** slip-road
At the **1st roundabout** take the **1st** exit into **LIGHTWATER BY-PASS (A322)**
Continue into **GUILDFORD ROAD**
At the **next roundabout (2)** take the **1st** exit into **BAGSHOT ROAD (A319)**
At the **1st mini-roundabout (3)** take the **1st** exit (turn left) into **HIGH STREET**
Cross over the small bridge and take the **1st** turning on the right into **CHERTSEY ROAD (A319)** following the signs for **CHERTSEY**
Continue into **CHOBHAM ROAD**
At the **next roundabout (4)** take the **1st** exit into **GUILDFORD ROAD (A320)**
At the **next roundabout (5)** take the **2nd** exit into **ST PETER'S WAY (A320)**
This leads to the **next roundabout (6)** which is Junction **11** of the **M25**
Follow the signs for the direction you wish to travel

Route 2 **Roundabouts (8)**

Leave the **M25** at Junction **12** follow the slip-road
Keep in the left hand slip-road which leads on to the **M3 LONDON**
Leave at the **1st** slip-road which is Junction **1** of the **M3**
At the **1st roundabout** take the **1st** exit into **STAINES ROAD WEST (A308)**
At the **3rd** traffic lights turn left into **WINDMILL ROAD** following the signs for signs **WALTON (A244)**
Continue into **UPPER HALLIFORD ROAD (A244)**
At the **roundabout (2)** take the **2nd** exit into **UPPER HALLIFORD BY-PASS**
At the **next roundabout (3)** take the **1st** exit into **GASTON BRIDGE ROAD**
At the **next roundabout (4)** take the **3rd** exit into **RUSSELL ROAD (B375)**
At the **mini-roundabout (5)** take the **2nd** exit (straight on) into **RUSSELL ROAD**
At the **next roundabout (6)** take the **2nd** exit (straight on) into **RENFREE WAY**
Continue into **CHERTSEY ROAD (B375)**
At the **next roundabout (7)** take the **1st** exit into **CHERTSEY BRIDGE ROAD**
Continue over the bridge into **BRIDGE ROAD**
At the traffic lights turn left into **WEIR ROAD** following the signs for the **M25**
Continue into **FORDWATER ROAD**
Continue into (straight ahead) **CHERTSEY ROAD**
At the **next roundabout (8)** take the **4th** exit into **ST PETER'S WAY (A317)**
This leads to the **next roundabout (9)** which is Junction **11** of the **M25**
Follow the signs for the direction you wish to travel

<u>JUNCTIONS 11 - 10</u> <u>(ANTI-CLOCKWISE)</u>

<u>**Route 1**</u>   <u>**Roundabouts (10)**</u>

Leave the **M25** at Junction **11** follow the slip-road
At the **1st roundabout** take the **1st** exit into **ST PETER'S WAY (A317)**
At the **next roundabout (2)** take the **3rd** exit into **WOBURN HILL (A317)**
At the **next roundabout (3)** take the **1st** exit into **WEYBRIDGE ROAD (A317)**
At the **1st mini-roundabout (4)** take **2nd** exit into **BALFOUR STREET**
At the **next mini-roundabout (5)** take the **1st** exit into **CHURCH STREET (A317)**
Continue into **HIGH STREET**   Continue into **MONUMENT HILL**
At the **next roundabout (6)** take the **2nd** exit (turn right)
Then keep left into **QUEENS ROAD (A317)** following the signs for <u>**BYFLEET**</u>
At the **roundabout (7)** take the **4th** exit into **SEVEN HILLS ROAD (B365)**
At the **next roundabout (8)** take the **2nd** exit (straight ahead)
At the traffic lights turn left into **BYFLEET ROAD (A245)**
At the **next roundabout (9)** take the **3rd** exit into **PORTSMOUTH ROAD (A3)** following the signs for the **M25**
Once on the **A3** leave at the **1st** slip-road
This leads to the **next roundabout (10)** which is Junction **10** of the **M25**
<u>**Follow the signs for the direction you wish to travel**</u>

<u>**Route 2**</u>   <u>**Roundabouts (8)**</u>

Leave the **M25** at Junction **11** follow the slip-road
At the **1st roundabout** take the **3rd** exit into **ST PETER'S WAY (A320)**
At the **next roundabout (2)** take the **1st** exit into **GUILDFORD ROAD (A320)**
At the **next roundabout (3)** take the **2nd** exit **(A320)**
At the **next roundabout (4)** take the **1st** exit (turn left) into **MARTYR'S LANE**
At the **T** Junction turn left into **WOODHAM LANE (A245)**
At the **next roundabout (5)** take the **2nd** exit into **SHEERWATER ROAD**
At the **next roundabout (6)** take the **1st** exit into **OLD WOKING ROAD**
Take the **1st** turning on the right into **OAKCROFT ROAD (B367)**
Continue into **COLDHARBOUR ROAD**   Continue into **UPSHOTT LANE**
At the **T** Junction turn left into **CHURCH HILL**   Continue into **THE PARADE**
Continue into **NEWARK LANE**
At the **T** Junction turn left into **HIGH STREET**
Continue into **PORTSMOUTH ROAD (B2215)**
At the **next roundabout (7)** take the **1st** exit on to the **A3** <u>**LONDON**</u>
Once on the **A3** leave at the **2nd** slip-road
This leads to the **next roundabout (8)** which is Junction **10** of the **M25**
<u>**Follow the signs for the direction you wish to travel**</u>

JUNCTIONS 10 - 9 (ANTI-CLOCKWISE)

Route 1 **Roundabouts (6)**

Leave the **M25** at Junction **10** follow the slip-road
At the **1st roundabout** take the **1st** exit (turn right) on to **PORTSMOUTH ROAD (A3)**
Leave at the **2nd** slip-road **(PAINSHILL JUNCTION)** following the signs for **COBHAM**
At the **next roundabout (2)** take the **3rd** exit (turn right) into **PORTSMOUTH ROAD (A245)**
At the **next roundabout (3)** take the **2nd** exit (straight ahead)
At the **next roundabout (4)** take the **2nd** exit (turn right) into **BETWEEN STREETS**
Continue into **HIGH STREET**
Continue into **MILL ROAD (A245)**
Continue into **STOKE ROAD** and continue over the railway bridge
Take the **1st** turning on the left (after garden centre) into **WOODLANDS LANE**
Continue into **WOODLANDS ROAD (A245)**
Then take the **1st** turning on the left into **OAKLAWN ROAD**
At the **next roundabout (5)** take the **2nd** exit (turn right) into **OXSHOTT ROAD (A244)**
This leads to the **next roundabout (6)** which is Junction **9** of the **M25**
Follow the signs for the direction you wish to travel

Route 2 **Roundabouts (4)**

Leave the **M25** at Junction **10** follow the slip-road
At the **1st roundabout** take the **1st** exit (turn left) into **PORTSMOUTH ROAD (A3)**
Continue into **ESHER BY-PASS (A3)**
Leave at the **3rd** slip-road following the signs for **M25 OXSHOTT**
At the **next roundabout (2)** take the **3rd** exit (turn right) into **COPSEM LANE (A244)**
Continue into **WARREN LANE (A244)**
Continue into **HIGH STREET (A244)**
Continue into **LEATHERHEAD ROAD (A244)**
Continue into **OXSHOTT ROAD (A244)**
At the **next roundabout (3)** take the **1st** exit (straight ahead)
This leads to the **next roundabout (4)** which is Junction **9** of the **M25**
Follow the signs for the direction you wish to travel

JUNCTIONS 9 - 8 (ANTI-CLOCKWISE)

Route 1 **Roundabouts (6)**

Leave the **M25** at Junction **9** follow the slip-road
At the **1st roundabout** take the **3rd** exit on to the **LEATHERHEAD BY-PASS**
At the **next roundabout (2)** take the **2nd** exit on to the **A243**
At the **next roundabout (3)** take the **2nd** exit (straight ahead)
At the **next roundabout (4)** take the **1st** exit into **REIGATE ROAD (B2033)**
Continue into **MILL WAY (B2033)** Continue into **LEECH LANE**
At the **T** Junction turn right into **HEADLEY COMMON ROAD (B2033)**
At the next **T** Junction turn right into **DORKING ROAD (B2032)**
Continue into **PEBBLE HILL ROAD** Continue into **STATION ROAD**
At the **next roundabout (5)** take the **1st** exit (turn left) into **REIGATE ROAD**
Continue into **MAIN ROAD (A25)** Continue into **BUCKLAND ROAD**
Continue into **WEST STREET** at the traffic lights turn left into **LONDON ROAD**
Keep left into **REIGATE HILL (A217)** following the signs for the **M25**
This leads to the **next roundabout (6)** which is Junction **8** of the **M25**
Follow the signs for the direction you wish to travel

Route 2 **Roundabouts (9)**

Leave the **M25** at Junction **9** follow the slip-road
At the **1st roundabout** take the **2nd** exit into **KINGSTON ROAD (A243)**
Continue into **LEATHERHEAD ROAD (A243)**
At the traffic lights turn right into **RUSHETT LANE (B280)**
Continue into **CHRISTCHURCH ROAD**
At the **next roundabout (2)** take the **2nd** exit
At the **next roundabout (3)** take the **2nd** exit
Continue into **WEST HILL** Continue into **WEST STREET**
At the traffic lights continue straight ahead into **HIGH STREET**
Keep right and at the **2nd** set of traffic lights continue right then immediate left into **UPPER HIGH STREET** following the signs to **REIGATE (A2022)**
Continue into **ALEXANDRA ROAD**
At the **next roundabout (4)** take the **1st** exit into **COLLEGE ROAD**
At the **next roundabout (5)** take the **2nd** exit (turn right) into **REIGATE ROAD**
At the **T** Junction turn right into **BRIGHTON ROAD (A217)**
At the **next roundabout (6)** take the **2nd** exit (straight ahead) **BRIGHTON ROAD**
At the **next roundabout (7)** take the **2nd** exit (straight ahead)
At the **next roundabout (8)** take the **2nd** exit (straight ahead)
This leads to the **next roundabout (9)** which is Junction **8** of the **M25**
Follow the signs for the direction you wish to travel

JUNCTIONS 8 - 7 (ANTI-CLOCKWISE)

Route 1 **Roundabouts (1)**

Leave the **M25** at Junction **8** follow the slip-road
At the **1st roundabout** take the **3rd** exit (turn right) into **REIGATE HILL**
Take the **1st** turning on the left into **GATTON BOTTOM**
At the **T** Junction (50yds) turn left again continuing along **GATTON BOTTOM**
At the **next T** Junction turn left into **LONDON ROAD NORTH (A23)**
Then take the **1st** turning on the right into **SHEPHERDS HILL (B2031)**
Continue into **ALDERSTEAD LANE** and at the top of the hill
Take the **1st** turning on the left into **DEAN LANE**
At the **T** Junction turn left into **BRIGHTON ROAD (A23)**
Keep in the left hand lane and follow on to the **M23**
Once on the **M23** this leads to Junction **7** of the **M25**
Follow the signs for the direction you wish to travel

Route 2 **Roundabouts (2)**

Leave the **M25** at Junction **8** follow the slip-road
At the **1st roundabout** take the **1st** exit (turn left) into **BRIGHTON ROAD (A217)**
At the **next roundabout (2)** take the **2nd** exit (turn right) into **BABYLON LANE**
At the **T** Junction turn left into **HIGH ROAD**
Take the **2nd** turning on the right into **HOGSCROSS LANE**
At the crossroads continue straight ahead into **STAR LANE**
At the **T** Junction turn right continuing along **STAR LANE**
At the traffic lights turn right into **BRIGHTON ROAD (A23)**
Keep in the left hand lane and follow on to the **M23**
Onceon the **M23** this leads to Junction **7** of the **M25**
Follow the signs for the direction you wish to travel

JUNCTIONS 7 - 6 (ANTI-CLOCKWISE)

Route 1 **Roundabouts (4)**

Leave the **M25** at Junction 7 follow the slip-road
Keep in the left hand lane and join the **M23** following the signs towards **CROYDON (M23)**
Then take the **1st** turning on the right into **DEAN LANE**
Keep right and at the **T** Junction turn left continuing along **DEAN LANE**
Continue into **ROOK LANE** Continue into **CHALDON ROAD**
At the **1st roundabout** take the **2nd** exit (straight ahead)
At the **next roundabout (2)** take the **2nd** exit (turn right) into **HIGH STREET**
Continue into **CHURCH ROAD** Continue into **CHURCH HILL**
Continue into **STATION AVENUE**
At the **next roundabout (3)** take the **2nd** exit (turn right) into **GODSTONE ROAD (A2030)**
At the **2nd** set of traffic lights turn right into **GODSTONE ROAD (A22)**
Continue into **GODSTONE HILL (A22)** following the signs for the **M25**
This leads to the **next roundabout (4)** which is Junction **6** of the **M25**
Follow the signs for the direction you wish to travel

Route 2 **Roundabouts (2)**

Leave the **M25** at Junction 7 follow the slip-road keep left and join the **A23**
At the traffic lights turn left into **STAR LANE**
Take the **2nd** turning on the left continuing along **STAR LANE**
At the crossroads continue straight ahead into **HOGSCROSS LANE**
At the **next** crossroads turn left into **HIGH ROAD**
Then take the **1st** turning on the left into **MARKEDGE LANE**
At the **T** Junction turn left into **GATTON BOTTOM**
At the **next T** Junction turn right then immediate left into **ROCKSHAW ROAD**
At the **next T** Junction turn left then turn **1st** right into **SPRING BOTTOM LANE**
At the **next T** Junction turn right into **WHITEHILL LANE** continue over the **M25**
Then take the **1st** turning on the left into **PLACE FARM ROAD**
Continue into **CHURCH LANE**
At the **T** Junction turn left into **GODSTONE ROAD (A25)**
Continue into **BLETCHINGLEY ROAD (A25)**
At the **T** Junction turn left then keep left into **HIGH STREET**
At the **1st roundabout** take the **1st** exit (straight ahead) into **GODSTONE HILL** following the signs for the **M25**
This leads to the **next roundabout (2)** which is Junction **6** of the **M25**
Follow the signs for the direction you wish to travel

JUNCTIONS 6 - 5 (ANTI-CLOCKWISE)

Route 1 **Roundabouts (2)**

Leave the **M25** at Junction **6** follow the slip-road
At the **1st roundabout** take the **3rd** exit on to **GODSTONE BY-PASS (A22)**
At the **next roundabout (2)** take the **1st** exit (turn left) into **OXTED ROAD (A25)**
Follow the **A25** (just keep on the main road) for **9** miles via **GODSTONE ROAD**
Continue into **WEST HILL**
Continue into **EAST HILL**
Continue into **WESTERHAM ROAD**
Continue into **HIGH STREET**
Continue into **MARKET SQUARE**
Continue into **VICARAGE HILL**
Continue into **QUEBEC SQUARE**
Continue into **BRASTED ROAD**
Continue into **WESTERHAM ROAD**
Continue into **HIGH STREET**
Continue into **MAIN ROAD**
This leads to Junction **5** of the **M25**
Follow the signs for the direction you wish to travel

Route 2 **Roundabouts (2)**

Leave the **M25** at Junction **6** follow the slip-road
At the **1st roundabout** take the **4th** exit into **GODSTONE HILL (B2235)**
At the **next roundabout (2)** take the **2nd** exit (turn left) into **OXTED ROAD (A225)**
Then take the **1st** turning on the left into **FLOWER LANE**
Continue into **GANGERS HILL**
At the **T** Junction turn right into **THE RIDGE**
At the next **T** Junction turn right then turn immediate left into **CLARKS LANE (B2024)**
Then take the **4th** turning on the left into **PILGRIMS WAY** following the signs for **WESTERHAM HILL**
At the **1st** crossroads continue straight ahead
At the **T** Junction turn right then immediate left continuing along **PILGRIMS WAY**
At the **next T** Junction turn right into **OVENDEN ROAD**
At the **next T** Junction turn right into **CHEVENING ROAD**
At the traffic lights turn left into **MAIN ROAD**
This leads to Junction **5** of the **M25**
Follow the signs for the direction you wish to travel

<u>JUNCTIONS 5 - 4 (ANTI-CLOCKWISE)</u>

<u>Route 1</u> **<u>Roundabouts (4)</u>**

Leave the **M25** at Junction **5** keeping to the right hand lane following the signs for **(A21) <u>SEVENOAKS</u> (M26)**
As you join the **M26** leave at the **1st** slip-road following the signs for **<u>WESTERHAM</u> (A25)** and leave at the **2nd** slip-road
At the **T** Junction turn left into **WESTERHAM ROAD (A25)**
Continue straight ahead into **MAIN ROAD**
At the traffic lights turn right into **CHEVENING ROAD (B2211)**
Continue into **SUNDRIDGE ROAD (B2211)**
At the **1st roundabout** take the **2nd** exit (straight ahead) into **POLHILL (A224)**
Continue into **LONDON ROAD (A224)**
At the **next roundabout (2)** take **3rd** exit into **ORPINGTON BY-PASS ROAD**
At the **next roundabout (3)** take the **5th** exit on to the **Motorway sliproad** following the signs for the **M25**
This leads to the **next roundabout (4)** which is Junction **4** of the **M25**
<u>Follow the signs for the direction you wish to travel</u>

<u>Route 2</u> **<u>Roundabouts (4)</u>**

Leave the **M25** at Junction **5** keeping to the right hand lane following the signs for **(A21) <u>SEVENOAKS</u> (M26)**
As you join the **M26** leave at the **1st** slip-road
Keep in the left hand slip-road following the signs for **<u>SEVENOAKS</u> (A21)**
Once on the **A21** leave at the **1st** slip-road continuing into **WESTERHAM ROAD (A25)**
Keep to the right hand lane and continue into **WORSHIPS HILL (A25)**
At the **1st mini-roundabout** take the **1st** exit (turn left)
At the **next mini-roundabout (2)** take the **1st** exit (straight ahead) into **LONDON ROAD**
Cross over the motorway bridge then turn right continuing along **LONDON ROAD**
Then take the **2nd** turning on the left into **FILSTON LANE**
Continue into **HIGH STREET**
At the **T** Junction turn left into **SHACKLANDS ROAD**
Then take the **1st** turning on the right into **CHELSFIELD LANE**
Continue into **SHOREHAM LANE**
Then take the **1st** turning on the left into **HEWITTS ROAD**
At the **next roundabout (3)** take the **1st** exit on to the **Motorway slip-road**
This leads to the **next roundabout (4)** which is Junction **4** of the **M25**
<u>Follow the signs for the direction you wish to travel</u>

<u>JUNCTIONS 4 - 3 (ANTI-CLOCKWISE)</u>

<u>Route 1</u> **<u>Roundabouts (4)</u>**

Leave the **M25** at Junction **4** follow the slip-road
At the **1st roundabout** take the **1st** exit (turn left)
At the **next roundabout (2)** take the **4th** exit into **COURT ROAD (A224)** following the signs for **<u>ORPINGTON</u>**
Continue into **CRAY AVENUE**
Continue into **SEVENOAKS WAY**
At the **next roundabout (3)** take the **3rd** exit following the signs for the **M20**
Keep to the right following the signs for **M20 <u>MAIDSTONE</u>**
As you continue around the roundabout take the **1st** exit on to the **SIDCUP BY-PASS (A20)** following the signs for **<u>MAIDSTONE</u> M25**
Once on the **A20** leave at the **1st** slip-road
This leads to the **next roundabout (4)** which is Junction **3** of the **M25**
<u>Follow the signs for the direction you wish to travel</u>

<u>Route 2</u> **<u>Roundabouts (6)</u>**

Leave the **M25** at Junction **4** follow the slip-road
At the **1st roundabout** take the **1st** exit (turn left)
At the **next roundabout (2)** take **1st** exit (turn left) into **ORPINGTON BY-PASS ROAD (A224)**
At the **next roundabout (3)** take the **1st** exit (turn left) into **SHACKLANDS ROAD**
Continue into **CASTLE FARM ROAD**
At the **T** Junction turn right into **REDLANDS LANE**
Continue into **CASTLE ROAD**
At the **next T** Junction turn left into **SHOREHAM ROAD (A225)**
Continue into **STATION ROAD (A225)**
Continue into **HIGH STREET (A225)**
Continue into **EYNSFORD ROAD (A225)**
At the **T** Junction turn left into **GORSE HILL (A20)**
At the **next roundabout (4)** take the **2nd** exit (straight ahead) into **LONDON ROAD**
At the **next roundabout (5)** take the **2nd** exit (straight ahead)
This leads to the **next roundabout (6)** which is Junction **3** of the **M25**
<u>Follow the signs for the direction you wish to travel</u>

JUNCTIONS 3 - 2 or 1b (ANTI-CLOCKWISE)

Route 1 **Roundabouts (6)**

Leave the **M25** at Junction **3** follow the slip-road
At the **1st roundabout** take the **5th** exit into **LONDON ROAD (A20)** following the signs for **FARNINGHAM (A20)**
At the **next roundabout (2)** take the **2nd** exit (straight on) into **LONDON ROAD**
Continue into **GORSE HILL**
At the **next roundabout (3)** take the **1st** exit (turn left)
Continue into **DARTFORD ROAD (A225)**
Continue into **MAIN ROAD (A225)**
Continue into **HAWLEY ROAD (A225)**
Keep right into **LOWFIELD STREET (A225)**
At the major traffic lights (crossroads) turn right into **PRINCES ROAD (A225)**
At the **next roundabout (4)** take the **2nd** exit (straight ahead)
This leads to the **next roundabout (5)** which is Junction **1b** of the **M25** by taking the **1st** exit you can join the **M25 ANTI-CLOCKWISE** here
If you intended to leave the **M25** at Junction **2** then take the **3rd** exit on to the **M25 Clockwise**
This will lead you to the **next roundabout (6)** which is Junction **2** of the **M25**
Follow the signs for the direction you wish to travel

Route 2 **Roundabouts (10)**

Leave the **M25** at Junction **3** follow the slip-road
At the **1st roundabout** take the **1st** exit (turn left) into **LONDON ROAD (B2173)**
Continue into **HIGH STREET**
At the **1st mini-roundabout (2)** take the **2nd** exit (straight ahead)
At the **next mini-roundabout (3)** take the **2nd** exit (turn right)
At the **next mini-roundabout (4)** take the **1st** exit into **BARTHOLOMEW WAY**
At the **next mini-roundabout (5)** take the **3rd** exit into **LONDON ROAD (B2173)**
As you pass the garage situated on the right turn right into **BIRCHWOOD ROAD**
At the **next mini-roundabout (6)** take the **2nd** exit (straight ahead) into **LEYTON CROSS ROAD**
At the **next roundabout (7)** take the **1st** exit (turn left) into **OAKFIELD LANE**
At the **next mini-roundabout (8)** take the **2nd** exit (turn right)
At the **next roundabout (9)** take the **3rd** exit on to the **DARTFORD BY-PASS (A2)** following the signs for **M25 DARTFORD TUNNEL**
Once on the **A2** leave at the **1st** slip-road
This leads to the **next roundabout (10)** which is Junction **2** of the **M25**
Follow the signs for the direction you wish to travel

JUNCTIONS 2 - 1b (ANTI-CLOCKWISE)

Route 1 **Roundabouts (2)**

Leave the **M25** at Junction **2** follow the slip-road
Keep in the middle lane
At the **1st roundabout** take the **2nd** exit keep to the left hand lane following the signs for **DARTFORD**
Keep to the left hand lane
This leads to the **next roundabout (2)** which is Junction **1b** of the **M25**
Follow the signs for the direction you wish to travel

Route 2 **Roundabouts (6)**

Leave the **M25** at Junction **2** follow the slip-road
At the **1st roundabout** take the **3rd** exit on to the **DARTFORD BY-PASS (A2)**
Once you are on the **DARTFORD BY-PASS (A2)** follow the signs for **BLUEWATER** and leave at the **1st** slip-road
Keep to the right hand lane
At the **next roundabout (2)** take the **2nd** exit following the signs for **DARTFORD**
At the **next roundabout (3)** take the **1st** exit (turn left) into **WATLING STREET**
At the **next roundabout (4)** take the **2nd** exit (straight ahead)
At the **next elongated roundabout (5)** take the **2nd** exit into **PRINCES ROAD**
This leads to the **next roundabout (6)** which is Junction **1b** of the **M25**
Follow the signs for the direction you wish to travel

Route 3 **Roundabouts (5)**

Leave the **M25** at Junction **2** follow the slip-road
At the **1st roundabout** take the **1st** exit on to the **DARTFORD BY-PASS (A2)** following the signs for **BEXLEY**
Once you are on the **DARTFORD BY-PASS (A2)** leave at the **1st** slip-road
At the **next roundabout (2)** take the **3rd** exit into **OLD BEXLEY LANE (A2081)** following the signs for **DARTFORD**
At the **next roundabout (3)** take the **2nd** exit (straight ahead) into **SHEPHERD'S LANE**
At the traffic lights turn right into **PRINCES ROAD (B2174)**
Continue through **3** sets of traffic lights
At the **next roundabout (4)** take the **2nd** exit (straight ahead)
This leads to the **next roundabout (5)** which is Junction **1b** of the **M25**
Follow the signs for the direction you wish to travel

JUNCTIONS 2 - 1a (ANTI-CLOCKWISE)

Route 1 **Roundabouts (7)**

Leave the **M25** at Junction **2** follow the slip-road
Keep in the middle lane
At the **1st roundabout** take the **2nd** exit following the signs for **DARTFORD**
Keep in the left hand lane this leads to the **next roundabout (2)** (Junction **1b**)
Take the **1st** exit (turn left) into **PRINCES ROAD**
At the **next roundabout (3)** take the **3rd** exit (turn right) into **PARK ROAD**
At the **mini-roundabout (4)** take the **2nd** exit (turn right) into **THE BRENT**
At the **next roundabout (5)** take the **2nd** exit (straight ahead)
Continue into **THE BRENT**
Continue into **LONDON ROAD**
At the traffic lights turn left into **COTTON LANE**
At the **next roundabout (6)** take the **2nd** exit (straight ahead)
This leads to the **next roundabout (7)** which is Junction **1a** of the **M25**
Follow the signs for the direction you wish to travel

Route 2 **Roundabouts (10)**

Leave the **M25** at Junction **2** follow the slip road
Keep in the right hand lane
At the **1st roundabout** take the **3rd** exit on to the **DARTFORD BY-PASS (A2)** following the signs for **BLUEWATER**
Once on the **(A2)** leave at the **1st** slip-road
At the **next roundabout (2)** take the **1st** exit into **ST CLEMENT'S WAY**
Keep to the right hand lane following the signs towards **CROSSWAYS**
At the **next roundabout (3)** take the **2nd** exit (straight ahead)
At the **next roundabout (4)** take the **2nd** exit (straight ahead)
At the **next roundabout (5)** take the **1st** exit (turn left) into **CROSSWAYS BOULEVARD**
At the **next roundabout (6)** take the **2nd** exit (straight ahead)
At the **next roundabout (7)** take the **2nd** exit (straight ahead)
At the **next roundabout (8)** take the **2nd** exit (straight ahead)
At the **next roundabout (9)** take the **3rd** exit (turn right)
This leads to the **next roundabout (10)** which is Junction **1a** of the **M25**
Follow the signs for the direction you wish to travel

FUTURE PUBLICATIONS

JUNCTION HOPPING the M1

JUNCTION HOPPING the M2

JUNCTION HOPPING the M3

JUNCTION HOPPING the M4

JUNCTION HOPPING the M5

JUNCTION HOPPING the M6

JUNCTION HOPPING BIRMINGHAM M5, M6, M42

JUNCTION HOPPING MANCHESTER M60

JUNCTION HOPPING the M11

JUNCTION HOPPING the M20

JUNCTION HOPPING the M23

JUNCTION HOPPING the M27

JUNCTION HOPPING the M62

AMONG OTHERS